Antonetta
An Immigrant's Story

Theresa Lombardi Magistro

Casa Lago Press
New Fairfield, CT

Diaspora
Volume 11

As "diaspora" is the dispersion or spread of people from their original homeland, this book series takes its name in the intellectual spirit of willful dispersion of subject matter and thought. It is dedicated to publishing those studies and creative works that in various and sundry ways either speak to or offer new methods of analysis and/or articulations of the Italian diaspora.

COVER PHOTO: Antonetta
COVER DESIGN: Teressa Healy

ISBN 978-1-955995-18-4
Library of Congress Control Number: 2026934995

CASA LAGO PRESS
New Fairfield, CT

For my mother

Antonetta, San Marco in Lamis, Italy, circa 1920

Antonio & Antonetta, Bronx, NY 1942

San Marco in Lamis, Italy

Table of Contents

ACKNOWLEDGEMENTS

Documenting the heartfelt memories of the past is sometimes easy, however, it is sometimes painful. I was supported and encouraged by several people important in my life. A team that understands tenderness and love. I thank my granddaughter Isabel who as a child continually asked me for more Antonetta stories. This book took years to write. During that time, I was in cancer treatment and, sadly, four of my siblings died.

Sitting on the beach in East Hampton, my sister, Nan (who has since passed away), and I compiled a list of the stories I needed to tell. I encouraged my eldest brother, Angelo (deceased), who had the longest memories to share what I could not know. Laughter was always a part of my eldest sister Grace's (deceased) reports when she recalled the adventures of our immigrant mishaps. I shared my written drafts with my brother, Lou (deceased), for his feedback, and benefited from many calls to my brother, George, for his perspective. Margo, my niece, read the drafts enthusiastically and provided valuable details.

I bestow the honorary title, Midwife of this book, to my Comare Bea Tusiani. She faithfully read my stories "hot off the press" providing valuable edits and with her supportive yet forceful encouragement to "keep writing." Michael Tusiani took time out of his demanding schedule with help in drawing a more accurate picture of the Sammarchese character. I fondly remember Professor Joseph Tusiani, a renowned international author, who, on a lovely afternoon in 2011, as we shared coffee in his home, smiling his disarming smile, he encouraged me to stay with my project. I asked him for permission to include one of his poems in my book. He reached for my writing pad and wrote: "Teresa you have my permission to reprint as many poems of mine as you wish, with great affection." Signed Joseph Tusiani. This, a treasured autograph indeed.

I especially thank Dr. Anthony Julian Tamburri and Casa Lago Press. Scholar and monumental cheerleader of Italian Americana, Anthony graciously supported me as a first-time author in my efforts to record my mother's memory and her experience in the Italian diaspora for posterity.

A very loud shoutout to my technology magicians gently dragging me into the twenty-first century: Maisy (granddaughter), Nina (granddaughter), Carey (niece) and of course, my daughter Meg who supported me through all my moments of panic. Meg was with me from the beginning nudging me along with her expertise and love. Carey not only instructed me in the uses of technology but enthusiastically served as my personal photographer. She is responsible for all the beautiful images in this book. My great niece and goddaughter, Teressa Healy, designed the book cover. She creatively used our passport cover from 1955. Yes, the joint passport document Mama and I were issued for my first voyage back to my roots. Finally, a big hug to Kate Magistro for proofreading the manuscript and her enthusiastic embrace of a culture not her own.

Antonetta would be thrilled to witness the power and love with which the women of her family came forward to help tell her story.

My first reader and enthusiastic motivator was my husband, Charles, who knew Mama and totally understood my need to have her remembered, remembered, and remembered. Our morning "coffee hour" discussions set the tone for my work. Thank you, Charles.

My endearing gratitude to all who helped me make these stories a permanent record for the future. Dear reader, we all have precious stories to tell, and I encourage you to start writing.

Preface

This book began as a collection of stories for great grandchildren yearning to know more about my mother whom they never met. The United States of America is a nation of immigrants. Each group brings its valued culture and traditions. Sometimes these are celebrated but sadly many are often forgotten with each new generation melding into a new time and place. Italian Americans have made substantial and long-lasting contributions to their new world.

This book is about one Italian family coming with enthusiasm and hope, and enjoying success in their adopted country. The central figure is Antonetta. She is a simple yet powerful woman who has much to teach us about appreciation for all the opportunities we have available to us in America. She teaches us about life and death, courage and hard work.

The book is written in three parts: background information, stories we love to share and, in the sharing, affectionately repeat again and again to each other, and finally, the lessons she taught us in facing death. The Appendix includes information significant to Antonetta's life.

We all have stories to tell and in the telling we share each group's unique spirit. I hope you enjoy meeting Antonetta and encourage you to document your own precious stories and valuable history. Although this is my mother's history, it documents the experience of a group of Italian immigrants from a different time. In sharing Antonetta's migration and diasporic experience and integration into American life as a productive and proud citizen, we are given an extraordinary role model. From her story, we witness firsthand the reality of achieving the "American Dream." Today, there are many who dream of a better life in America, and perhaps these stories can provide insight into the possibilities for successful transitions to a new country and a new world.

PART ONE

Background

Antonia Vincitorio – Antonetta Vincitorio Lombardi was born in 1901 and died 1982. Who was this extraordinary woman raised without parents in Puglia, a southern region, with little but sunshine and fertile land? For the poor, the Italy of the early 1900s was very different from the Italy later visited by her children, grandchildren and great grandchildren. She began her life with no family and ended it with the enduring devotion of her six surviving children, their spouses, many grandchildren and three great grandchildren. Her story is our history. What was the source of the strength and optimism for this courageous woman who faced the early years of childhood without family on the *massaria*, the farm, to work for her keep from the age of nine? This is the story of Antonetta's migration, her Italian diasporic experience into a world anchored in her prayers and imagined in dreams, in a new world, in a land of hope and opportunity.

As a young child my granddaughter, Isabel, would love to hear Antonetta stories; stories about the great grandmother whom she never met. Maisy, another great granddaughter chose Antonetta as a first-grade genealogy project wearing Mama's red Christmas apron and showing her classmates an old wooden bowl and antique pasta cutter, treasures saved from the past, from the life of her Italian great grandmother. My daughter, Meg reminisces about this fierce grandmother who would glide her hands through a bucket of crabs that she and brother, Paul and cousin, Marco, fished out of the East Hampton waters on wondrous summer days. She was amazed. "Why was it that those crabs did not dare to bite Grandma?" This memoir is for the children who did not know Mama but whose lives are forever strengthened by the powerful genetic connection to this tiny woman born in poverty from a different culture, country and century. Telling her story helps me "make sense of life." Where do we find meaning? How do we cope with our disappointments and celebrate our blessings?

THE STORY BEGINS

Antonetta shared her memories. She often recalled stories of the loss of her parents as a young child and her early years growing up on a farm without family. As a teenager she lived with and worked for the Ciavarella family. They became her adopted family for whom she had a deep affection and strong bond throughout her life.

Immigration documents required for travel to America in 1929 identify Mama as Antonia Vincitorio. Italian records always identify a woman by her maiden name. She was born on February 22, 1901, in the town of San Marco in Lamis, located in the Province of Foggia in Puglia on the Adriatic Coast of Italy. The document shows her father's name as Michelangelo Vincitorio and her mother's, Maria Teresa Mimmo. Antonetta's profession is listed as *casalinga*, housewife. She is described as small in stature having brown eyes, chestnut hair and colorful cheeks.

What is most compelling about Mama's story is the telling of this tiny woman from a simple peasant background who became a giant to those who knew and loved her. Although she had little of material value, Mama was armed with the power of love and the strength in her Catholic faith. She was a realistic optimist. Antonetta, tiny Antonia, was given precious little as a child. As often told, her Christmas gifts were an orange or a few nuts. Her only measure of wealth was her parents' love. And this was taken from her in childhood at a time when medical care was severely limited, especially for the poor of Southern Italy. There were few doctors, no antibiotics or other medicines and no hospital in the region where she lived. She had little, but she was not fearful or resentful. Never complaining about the difficult challenges she faced in her life: orphaned at an early age, the death of three daughters, the many economic hardships she faced through the *miseria,* poverty, in Italy, the Great Depression in America, two world wars, the worry of her adored sons serving in the military; Angelo in World War II, Lou in the Korean War and George in Germany during the late 1950s, least they would be wounded or worse. This worry was not misplaced. Papa had served in World War I and barely escaped with his life. He was wounded and carried shrapnel in his leg for the rest of his life.

In the 1960s she went through another time of worry because her grandson, Billy A was serving in Vietnam.

Mama lived with economic insecurity. Papa was a laborer (plasterer) whose cash flow was erratic. "La vita e una vita di sacrifici." Life is a one of sacrifices was her response to the difficulties she faced. She did not think of herself as a victim or deprived. For her life's challenges had a higher meaning that enabled her to appreciate the gifts she was given. Mama was forever positive and unshaken. She was not afraid of life, and she was not afraid of strangers. She had a deep religious faith that strengthened her spirit. She taught us that most people are good, and she was forever grateful to those she encountered who helped her throughout her life.

Let's begin with the story of this fearless pilgrim. Her life's journey was so very different from her offspring. In March 2013 my husband, Charles, and I traveled back to her birthplace but this time our mission was to search official documents, to gather what facts that might be available in the Italian church and municipal records documenting her early years.

I faced this mission with some trepidation. I was warned, yes warned, in almost angry tones by one of my sisters and two brothers not to do this. They said there were "secrets," things Mama did not want others to know. One of her children thought that she might have been an illegitimate child that birth records would show no names of her mother and father. Perhaps they thought this would tarnish her image. What difference would it make? But how could this be? She spoke so lovingly of her parents. She kept them alive for me in her stories. Why, she even gave me a pair of primitively whittled castanets, saying her father had made them many years before. I was determined to know more. Little is known about Mama's early years except for what she shared with us. We knew that her parents both died when she was young. An orphan, she was sent to live on a farm. Who made this decision for her? Who were those who cared for her as a young child? How did she get to that particular farm? Where was the farm? We didn't ask and now we don't know.

She always had a strong affection for Luigi Nitto, a farmer. A special person we were instructed to visit whenever one of us traveled back to San Marco. What role did he play in her life? It was all so confusing. Mama never tired of saying that two of her children were named after her parents. As is the Italian custom the first-born children are given the names of their paternal grandparents. And so, my brother, Angelo and sister, Grace are named after Papa's parents. I was named after Mama's mother, MariaTeresa. Unfortunately, the teachers at Public School 13 in the Bronx felt that Teresa, the Italian spelling of my name, was incorrect and changed it to Theresa. Why didn't anyone ever question that change? Perhaps because none of those educators were Italian. I wonder? Mama also said that my brother Lou, Luigi, who always insisted that he was her favorite child, was named after her father. This is curious because her documents list her father as Michelangelo, a name I do not remember her sharing with us. Luigi is even listed as her father's name on her death certificate. Was Luigi her father on the farm?

As a teenager Antonetta left the farm. Perhaps it was no longer appropriate for a teenage girl to live and work side-by-side with the mostly male farm workers. In Italy at that time there were strict rules and customs regarding the need for a young woman to always be chaperoned in mixed company. And so, she went to live in the village with the Chiavarella family. This family became her family. Za Zia, Angelina, was the mother of the house and Mama considered her a sister. Angelina's children, Lena, Pasquale, Maria Christina and Luigi, became her nieces and nephews. A family I remember with affection. Mama and I stayed with the Chiavarellas for two months when we traveled to Italy in 1955. It was then I learned that when the baby Luigi was born, at the same time of my brother Angelo's birth, Mama saved his life by nursing both babies. Za Zia was ill after his birth and couldn't feed her own baby." Milk mothers" were not unusual at the time. Remember, bottle feeding was not available in those years. Luigi became a tall handsome man and joked saying it was Mama's milk that made him so big and strong. He lovingly called her *Zia Menena,* tiny aunt. Yes, she was indeed tiny, less than five feet tall.

RESEARCHING HER HISTORY

Back to our document hunt in San Marco. On a cold rainy morning, two days after Easter in 2013, thanks to the special arrangements made by our dear 93-year-old cousin Maria, we met Filomena Bisceglia, city clerk at the *Municipio,* City Hall. Maria, our only surviving first cousin and daughter of Zio Giuseppe, my father's older brother, had asked a special favor for her cousin Teresa coming all the way from America searching for family records. Our cousin, Grazia, Maria's daughter, lovingly and patiently served as our guide, our *consiglieri,* to uncover the past at the village's historic town hall. At the old structure with its oversized doors and brooding demeanor, the same building that stood there at the time of our parent's birth. As we entered, we were greeted with a stern look from the tired bureaucrat sitting behind the counter who didn't seem the least bit interested in why these three people were politely standing before him waiting for his attention.

After several long minutes, Grazia spoke and inquired about where we might find the City Clerk, stating that we had an appointment with her that morning. With a frown, he pointed to a back room. We walked through several cluttered offices, with desks full of unruly piles of paper, to find the dignified and charming Filomena wearing a soft blue cashmere sweater casually draped over her shoulders.

Filomena was an elegant middle-aged woman with warm gentle eyes and the erect posture of an aristocrat. She was not at all the bureaucrat I feared awaiting my special task that morning. She greeted us warmly with a kiss on each cheek, as is the custom in Italy, and inquired about our cousin, Maria. Grazia gave her *Pasqua*, Easter, wishes and asked about her family. She spoke about her children and was especially proud of her son, who was in seminary, studying for the priesthood. She spoke affectionately about our dear deceased cousin, Don Angelo and his life-long ministry in the Catholic church of San Antonio Abate in that town. In Italy, personal conversation usually precedes serious business. We learned that Filomena was born in San Marco and also has a house in Borgo Celano, a mountaintop summer community overlooking the beautiful Gargano. Borgo Celano is a hamlet full of special memories, of family gatherings with our *cugini*, cousins on our trips back to Italy, our trips back to our roots. The empathetic Filomena looked into my eyes, and she immediately understood my emotional turmoil. She knew I was here on a mission of love and with a gentle touch assured me that I was in kind hands. She was there to help.

With copies of the documents that accompanied our parents to America, Filomena began her search through the old dusty records to find the history of our mother. I came prepared with a copy of Mama's identity card issued in San Marco when she left Italy in May 1929 listing the names of both her parents. She first found my grandfather's birth record and then my grandmother's.

They were preserved in an unusual, oversized green, cloth-covered book held together by an ancient screw needing a particular key to separate the pages in order to make copies. The past was all at once opened to me. I did have a grandmother and grandfather after all! Mama's stories about her father's death came alive and jumped off the page at me. Clearly the fact was he died, as she told us, in 1905 when Antonetta was only four years old. I was overwhelmed. I fought back the tears and heard my mother's voice, *cara figlia*, dear daughter.

As was the practice, the document was amended to show my grandfather's death and its cause, pneumonia, with the doctor's signature authenticating the fact. Michelangelo was born in 1854 and was 47 when Mama was born. Mama told us that her parents had other children, but they all died and she was the only surviving child. Some members of our family were not confident about Mama's recollection of her early years and the information about her parents. Yes, her birth certificate listed her mother, Maria Teresa Mimmo. She was born on May 27, 1858 and died on June 19, 1910. Antonetta was only nine years old. The documents revealed she had a sister who also died in 1910. The outbreak of Cholera in Italy in that year was the probable cause of both deaths.

Her home address Via Madonna Incoronata #71. Energized, I returned home armed with copies of the birth certificates for my parents, grandparents and our two eldest siblings, Angelo and Grazia (Grace, we always called her by her English name) who were both born in Italy.

I was eager to share my findings with the family. Mama's

stories were real. She was the beloved daughter who was a gift to her parents in their later years. I thought of Mama and Papa. I was the youngest of the family, "the change-of-life baby," born to them when she was 44 and he was 50. Fortunately, they lived a better life in America. Their children would survive the challenges of giving birth at home without medical care and the ravages of poverty. I often think about how the love she received for those few short years was enough to strengthen and sustain her for a lifetime. This must have been a powerful bond, and profound love. Her stories were true. She shared her childhood memories about work on the farm and life in the small village and the richness of the religious traditions. The Catholic faith where forgiveness and renewal were ongoing, and where religious practices and celebrations sustained fortitude and hope.

I still have so many questions. What were the early years of life like for this little girl whose father died when she was four and her mother died when she was nine with no surviving family members to take care of her? Did she go to school? We learned she did. This may have been before her mother died while she still lived in the village. Mama said she went to school until the third grade. Just think, barely enough education to enable her to read and write.

However, she was literate and was the one the *paesans,* her Sammarches friends, would ask to write letters to communicate with their families in Italy. Can you imagine a girl with just a third-grade education would become the scribe for an immigrant community? Well, the truth is, Mama assumed this important role in her community.

After her mother's death how did the transition from life in the village to life on the farm evolve? What was the reality of her farm life? Where did she sleep? Who bought her clothes? Who took care of her? Mama spoke about her years on the farm with affection.

She spoke about the little tasks she was given in the

kitchen helping to prepare meals for the farm workers. She reminisced how she stood on a little box to reach the table where she accomplished her assigned tasks. I am sure it was here she learned to be such an extraordinary cook. She spoke about the summertime when she was assigned, armed with her little basket and a knife, to sell and peel prickly pears at the side of the country road. Years later Mama taught her children how to carefully cut away the skin so that we did not get pinched by the sharp needles of the fruit's outer skin. Each time she peeled the prickly pears she repeated the story. Each time she did, I loved hearing it.

I couldn't imagine losing my home, having to earn my keep when I was only nine years old. Mama remembered the kindness of those with whom she lived on that farm. She never expressed anger about her loss and suffering at such an early age. Being a deeply religious person, she believed that each life had a plan, one not always easily understood but one with a serious intention. The pain in her life was faced with a shrug of her shoulders and the words "what are you going to do?" She said this not with a feeling of being overpowered by a greater force but with a faith in life's meaning. For her marriage to the tall, handsome man she loved, the blessing of her many children and a life in a new land, and a country full of opportunities carried her through the moments of sadness. Yes, sadness but not despair.

SAMMARCHESE HOUSES

After spending several hours at City Hall with Charles and Grazia we walked a short distance down steep stone steps to the first house Antonio and Antonetta lived in as husband and wife. We knew the name of this street because it was recorded on their municipal records. Filomena walked out of the *Municipio* with us and pointed to the location of the newlyweds' home. As I looked at the small stone building, I was reminded of my mother's story about the birth of her first child, my brother Angelo. On that freezing January day my father was so thrilled with his son's birth that he insisted on wrapping him up and taking him out to show family and friends his beautiful child. I picture Papa, "Tough Tony" as his children affectionately refer to him, in all of his pride and excitement carrying Angelo through those narrow ancient streets bursting with joy at the beginning of his large family; the first born of three boys and six girls.

The documents showed another address, Via Boux (later spelled Via Bux). Our brother Angelo always remembered as his first house, it was a short distance away. Number 6 was the house in which Mama, Angelo and Grace lived when Papa emigrated to America. Alone and separated from his little family, he was working and preparing the way for them to come to America, to begin a new life where they would find economic opportunity and a bright future. The stone house, attached to others on both sides, was really just one room with a fireplace for warmth and cooking, no windows, no electricity, no running water with a large front portal for light during the daytime.

La Chiesa Madre – The Mother Church

We then walked just one block to *La Chiesa Madre*, the Mother Church: the oldest church in San Marco. The same church attended on that June day when Antonetta and Antonio were married. The church was closed when we arrived. I found some workmen busy at a nearby building and inquired about the church. One of them put down his tools and told me that I might find the priest in another building. He gave me directions and even walked me there himself. He rang the bell but there was no answer. Don Matteo was not home. How was I to find the church records which would give me more precious information about Antonetta's life? My disappointment must have been obvious to this man who was standing so close to me. He asked me what I was doing there.

Dear reader, we were fortunate to grow up learning to speak both English and the Sammarchese dialect enabling us to communicate in our home village. I explained that I had come from America to see the church in which my parents were married more than 90 years before. With a gentle smile he told me to wait. He knew a woman who had the keys to the church. Amelia was a little old woman in tattered clothes and old worn slippers, missing teeth and an energetic sparkle in her eyes. She gave me a kiss, on both cheeks, of course, and proudly said that she would open the church for us. Grazia, our loving cousin, introduced herself as Don Angelo Lombardi's niece and told her the reason for our visit.

Amelia opened the huge wooden door which had a smaller opening for us to step through and guided us through the dark marble hall. She announced that she first had to show us something special and took us to the sacristy where she pointed to a wall of wooden wardrobes, a long, tall closet where the priest's vestments were stored, including, she informed us, those worn by our very own cousin, dear Don Angelo. When, as a local priest, he said Mass in that church he used these same wardrobes. Yet another thread connecting us to this awesome spiritual home.

We then walked through the small side door, where priests entered the church, and we experienced a magnificent chapel. This was constructed all in wood behind the main altar. We were told that the church was dedicated in the early 1800s and that this original wooden chapel remained in the rear but was later replaced by the extraordinary marble altar and the two side chapels. I walked down the center aisle of La Chiesa Madre and wondered what my parents felt making their vows in this peaceful space beginning a new life together. What was life like for them in this village? What were their hopes? What were their dreams? Could they have imagined that they would go to a new land, begin a new life and leave a large family as the legacy of their love?

I walked out of the church, and I felt their embrace. I heard, *cara figlia*, dear daughter. I was strengthened by the force of the many nurturing years, the affection and the pride they both took in their children and grandchildren. The family, they announced in the later years, as their greatest treasure and source of wealth.

Standing outside the church, I knew that I had to return. I had to come again when I could find the information I was seeking. But as I entered the church square, I looked up to the sky, and I was shaken by another memory. A story that Angelo often enjoyed telling about his very first job. Jobs were important in our family. We were instilled with the belief that finding work was both a blessing and a responsibility. Something that was not always a given for the poor peasants of Southern Italy. As a young child, Angelo did find a job. He served as the bell ringer for this church. He was only about five or six years old and too small to get on the knot of the thick hemp rope himself to pull ringing the bell announcing the time for Mass to all the villagers. With the priest's help he energetically rang that bell. The one lira that he earned, Italian currency of the time, was proudly given to Mama.

In the 1920's this one lira was worth approximately 0.05 cents! With this he was supplementing the meager family income. At that time each lira was dear, especially for Mama, alone with two children and little money. I wonder what that lira could buy.

LIFE BEGINS IN AMERICA

Papa had first come to America in about 1913 as a young single man in search of his fortune. Due to the political crisis in Europe and World War I, he was conscripted into the army and had to return to Italy to serve in the Italian army. At that time, America and Italy were allies, fighting the same enemies. After the war he returned to San Marco and married

Mama. In 1923 and after the birth of his two children Papa knew there was little hope for survival in the hills of Puglia. Economic conditions in Italy were dire. Providing food for even a small family had been a desperate challenge. Thus, with Italy devastated by the war, he returned to America to earn money and to tap into the many resources that were not available to him in his native land. Our father left in search of a better life for his wife and children. Imagine what it took for those peasants to leave their families and culture in order to find work opportunities in a new country. He labored hard and lived in a boarding house. He was separated from those he loved for six long years until he could legally send for his wife and children to join him in America.

After arriving in New York Harbor and processed at Ellis Island, he was prepared to face the opportunities in his adopted country. He was ready to find work and begin to build a new life in the Bronx. He chose the Bronx because other *paesans* preceded him to America and reported back on the job possibilities awaiting those with "strong backs" and determination to succeed. He was forced to adapt to different kinds of work in a new environment, unlike anything he did in the past.

He was eager to change his low paying job in San Marco driving a horse-drawn wagon, transporting produce from his brothers' farm to the village each day. As with many immigrants, life in the new world drastically changed their lives in a desperate quest for survival.

After many years in America the time had come for Antonetta to return to Italy. She emigrated to America in 1929 and now in 1955 with money she had carefully saved, she planned her journey back. What motivated her to make this decision? What would she see; who would she see? As the baby of the family, I was the fortunate child chosen to join Mama on her trip. This voyage back forever changed my life. Arrangements were made and we were ready. We departed from New York City in August to cross the Atlantic Ocean to the old country, the land of all the air mail letters on the flimsy blue paper, the land of the many dinnertime stories, the land of my ancestors.

THE VOYAGE

The decision was made to travel by ship. Passage was booked on the newly built Italian ocean liner, the Cristoforo Columbo, the sister ship of the tragic Andrea Doria. I remember seeing that fatal ship at sea gracefully passing us like a giant fin, gliding on an angle in the gigantic Atlantic Ocean. I recalled the terror at hearing the reports of its tragic sinking just a year later.

In our new clothes, shiny shoes and corsage pinned to my mother's dress we waved goodbye to our family and friends standing on the pier seeing us off. Music played and Mama looked at me *coraggio,* courage she whispered. Was she thinking of her first transatlantic crossing those 26 years ago?

Traveling by ship was an enchanting eight-day excursion on an enormous floating hotel. The ocean voyage immersed me in a newfound wonderland. Growing up in a large family of immigrant parents this "hotel' experience was certainly not part of my life. A whole new world of unknown possibilities was unfolding before me. In truth, traveling across the awesome Atlantic was a bit scary. But this was not the case for Antonetta. She walked across the gangplank with the grace and confidence of a seasoned traveler. She knew who she was and where she was going. This was merely a means to an end, and she certainly would enjoy every treat in store for us.

The ship was huge and magnificent. For me it was the fairytale castle of my childhood fantasies. Of the ship's three classes, we traveled third. No matter, it was far more elegant than anything I had ever experienced. People strolled along the deck in beautiful clothes, handsome sailors charmed us with ongoing attention, and I was the princess of the ship. The dining room was elegant. We ate delicious meals on white linen tablecloths with real china and sparkling glassware. There was not a single jelly glass on that table. Jars, especially jelly jars because of their shape and size were often the glassware of choice back in the Bronx. Mama sat erect and was very much at home in this elegant setting, she was the one being served rather than the one serving. Just imagine how it must have felt for Antonetta to have eight days of leisure time to say her rosaries and have all our needs met by others. This was hardly her experience of everyday life in the Bronx. We played shuffleboard, I went swimming in the circular pool wearing my new green bikini bathing suit and we danced to the music in the bewitching formal ballroom.

Mama being Mama, she found that we could go to Mass in the beautiful second-class chapel each morning rather than hearing Mass in the far side of the third-class dining room. This jewel of a chapel had a most extraordinary oil painting of the Madonna and Child. The priest was gentle and kind and welcomed us to Mass each day. I often wonder how Antonetta found her way to the chapel. Who told her about it, how did she find it? I only know that we climbed the correct staircase and found ourselves very much at home in this precious space. I was inspired by the painting and have had an attachment to *La Madonna* ever since. I now have a collection that includes images of strong spiritual women from many countries and cultures. And I am reminded of the strong woman I accompanied on that massive ship.

The one startling and frightening experience was the ship's drill. With the sound of an alarm, we donned our life jackets and were directed to assigned stations on the deck silently standing by the rails where lifeboats hung over the deep, dark blue, ocean water. The whole ship was on alert, with anxious stares as we stood there in complete silence waiting for the signal to return to our cabins. After seeing the 1953 film *Titanic* I was sure this was our tragic end. Mama and all the adults were serious. She did not smile but carefully followed directions. All instructions were in both English and Italian. She whispered a special blessing as we slowly walked down the stairs at the completion of the drill.

Our cabin was small but there was enough room for our luggage. I was thrilled because I finally slept in a bunk bed. The top bunk was mine and I loved being Mama's room-mate. Just the two of us together for all those days at sea.

The Arrival

On the eighth day we arrived in the port of Naples. The very same port Antonetta sailed from with her two firstborn children many years before. There was a lot of commotion and long lines until we finally left the ship. We spent a short time in Naples waiting for the train to Foggia and then took a bus to the village of San Marco. I am amazed that we navigated this return ourselves. I guess Antonetta knew exactly where she was going. No problem for her. I don't remember much about this trip across the country to Puglia. Some images are so clear – I can almost feel the warm Italian sun on my skin – and some are not. I do remember being frightened by the bombed-out buildings near the train station in Foggia. I heard about the war from my parents and studied about it in history class, but the reality of the actual destruction was a new experience for me. *"La Guerra,"* the war was the only comment made as we witnessed the destruction. Why were there still so many bombed out buildings almost a decade later? I soon learned of the economic burdens faced by the Italians during this period.

The packages Mama sent to our cousins came to mind. Parcels carefully wrapped in cloth and sewn together – Antonetta's version of durable wrapping to withstand rough handling she was sure would accompany their transport across the Atlantic. These packages were carried during the post-war years to the post office filled with clothing and medicine. The very packages our cousin Maria gratefully remembered each time we made our way back to be with her.

My first sights upon our arrival in the Sammarchese town square were startling – unfolding like a movie set. There were few cars, many bikes, vespas, motorcycles and the astonishing sight of donkeys meandering along the village streets carrying oversized bundles on both sides with baskets full of food and pottery containers. I saw a woman walking with a flat board securely placed on her head with freshly baked loaves of bread being gracefully carried home from one of the town's ovens. A bubbling fountain greeted us on that hot August day. The town had a scent, I can still recall. One hard to describe, it combined a freshness of country air and yet an unknown odor of something smoky and ancient at the same time. Women were wearing full length black dresses carrying heavy packages on their heads. There were no shopping carts in this village. I saw children, some of whom also dressed all in black, mourning a loved one. I remember their shiny faces with rosy cheeks. I was told that their cheeks were so rosy because they ate the crust of homemade bread. The boys all wore short pants, and the little girls wore big white bows in their hair. Antonetta approached someone who looked familiar. All of a sudden there were screeches and yells and hugs and kisses and tears. She found an old friend all these years later. How did this happen? Mama was home again. Needless to say, the whole town got involved in the encounter. A pilgrim returned from the new world! This was certainly a celebration. A crowd formed and a parade of locals accompanied us through the narrow stone streets, passing many ancient stone structures to *ZaZia's*, auntie, house on Via del Purgatorio, today renamed Via Giosue Carducci.

ZaZia, an affectionate term for sweet aunt, whom Mama considered her sister, took Antonetta in when she was a young teenager to work as a nanny for her children. For Italians, when a person comes to live and work in your home, that person ceases to be a stranger and becomes a member of the family. They often do not earn a wage but inherit a strong bond, a family.

We walked up the steep stone steps on the side of the building to ZaZia's house. It consisted of two large rooms – one with a huge fireplace, for cooking and heat, and a balcony. The balcony included a small cooking alcove, So many meals came from such a small space. Each room had a very large bed and tables and chairs. There was no living room, no electricity and no plumbing. For a ten-year-old it felt like camping outside/inside. We went to the village wells for water and used a discreetly hidden chamber pot in a storage closet on the outside steps. This was a BIG change for me. As the months passed the cold weather brought another interesting accommodation. Hot coals were placed in a *brasiere*, a copper circular pan about two feet in diameter with a raised flat edge for our feet about four inches from the floor – kind of a platform or lip designed to place our feet so that our toes were kept warm while stories of the war were told and prayers were offered as we sat on chairs in a circle. This seemed so natural for Mama who didn't miss the luxury of centralized heating she came to enjoy in her house in America. I however, found this to be thrilling – a campfire on the floor, inside a house!

LIFE IN THE VILLAGE

Everything was different in San Marco. It was an adventure. The village is in a valley surrounded by beautiful mountains that change color with the movement of the sun. Everything is made of stone. The only thing green grows in fanciful clay pots filled with flowers and herbs seen on the balconies. Grass and trees are in *La Villa,* the central park. This is the focal point of the village where the excitement of daily life unfolds each afternoon for *passaggio,* the after dinner and after nap village walk. An essential practice for intense people-watching. This is a time-honored tradition which takes a bit of getting used to for an American. But on later visits as a woman I must admit the sensuous stares stirred a welcomed awakening.

The sounds are also different. There are animals, dogs, cats, pigs, sheep, donkeys and many loud people. The whole town comes out. The children are running screaming to their playmates, women are talking excitedly, the men are smoking cigars and smiling contentedly. Then the magnificent church bells begin their disarming chants. There are many churches in this small town. Mass is about to begin. However, the lovers do not respond to the signal. They occupy a dedicated space we call "lovers' lane," kissing passionately in exaggerated embraces for all to see. What fun!

Out of nowhere comes a funeral procession. I had never seen anything quite like this. The ornate casket is carried in a shiny black horse-drawn wagon. The sides of the wagon are glass for clear view of the closed casket decorated with an intricate black and silver motif. The horses prance majestically wearing tall, plumed crowns. Following the casket are two rows of men wearing white robes with white hoods. Oh no, I thought the Klan had landed. It was scary. A priest and altar boys in full regalia were followed by a brass band playing soulful music and then family and friends of the deceased walked solemnly through the streets of San Marco winding up to the village cemetery.

This was so unusual for me but so familiar to Mama. In Italy death is an integral part of life and is celebrated in all its richness and drama. Every aspect of human existence was taken seriously and had profound importance in this country, whether it was preparing a meal or coming to terms with the ultimate meaning of life. How did Antonetta adjust to America after growing up in a place where the reality of everyday life was so different?

Although we spent most of our time with ZaZia and her children, we did visit with Papa's family. Mama had a comfortable relationship with her in-laws and spent endless hours catching up on all that couldn't be included in the many letters that crossed the Atlantic. Although Papa was estranged from his brothers, Mama was not.

During the warm months, Lombardi relatives lived in Borgo Celano, a hamlet just about a mile up the mountain from San Marco. Life here is tranquil and calm. It was here that I first met my dear cousin Maria, her husband Pasquale, and her loving children: Palma, Archangela, Grazia and Matteo. The youngest son, Giuseppe, was not yet born. I have maintained a close and loving relationship with these cousins and their children to this day.

Borgo Celano's geography is its gift. Situated up the mountain from San Marco it is cool and offers beautiful views of the coastal beaches of the Gargano as well as the fertile farmlands seen in the plateau below. The sounds of cowbells are often heard when exploring the surrounding hills. And of course, prayers and chants from the solemn 10th century monastery, San Matteo, anchor your soul to the spirit of the land, to its people and their God. Borgo Celano has become the magnet for all of us, the American cousins who return to the beguiling land and our Italian roots. To our loving family. Here we celebrate our history, our culture, and those who will always be in our hearts.

Theresa & Italian Cugini Archangela,
Grazia, Matteo, Palma Iantoschi
Borgo Celano, Italy 1955

Cugini Celebrating a Delicious Meal
Pasquale, Grazia, Michele, Meg, Charles, Lucia (standing),
Don Angelo, Maria, Adina (standing),
Leticia, Giuseppe, Daniele
Borgo Celano, Italy 1984.

PART TWO

Antonetta's Stories

The Chicken and the Buttons

This Antonetta story was told by my brother Angelo, the eldest of the family born in Italy where he lived with Mama and his baby sister, Grace, until he came to America at the age of eight to be reunited with Papa. Before I start the story background information is needed to fully appreciate the significance of the two buttons. Italy suffered severe economic conditions following WWI with the people of Southern Italy experiencing the greatest hardship. Papa had come to America as a teen and was conscripted during WWI. He left the United States and served in the Italian army since the two countries were allies at the time. After Papa served in the Italian army and his marriage and the birth of his two children, he again left Italy and returned to America. This difficult decision was made for economic survival, leaving Mama, Angelo (age two) and Grace (a newborn) in San Marco. He knew work was available for him in the United States and the hope of a better life across the Atlantic Ocean was real for his little family.

Changes in the new Immigration Act of 1924 (Johnson Reed Act) which then limited the number of immigrants who could be admitted from any country to two percent of the number of people from that country who were already in the United States in 1890. Since "the largest immigrant wave from Southern Europe came between 1890 and 1915" this substantially cutback the number that could be admitted from Italy after the adoption of this new law. Papa was separated from his family and Mama faced life alone with two small children in Italy with few resources. It was not until 1929 that Papa, after securing his American citizenship, meeting other requirements enabled Mama, Angelo and Grace to come to America after a six-year separation filled with sacrifice and dreams of a better life.

    What was life like for Antonetta and two young children in this little village in the valley with few resources? Their house, located at #6 Via Boux (now spelled Via Bux), was just one room in a small stone building in a row of houses. There were no windows on either side because the structure was attached. Without electricity the only daylight came from a large entrance door. Kerosene lamps, candles and the fireplace were used for interior lighting. The sparse room included a bed, table, chairs and the fireplace for heating and cooking. Also, there was no running water. Therefore, the villagers had to go to the town wells to get water for their daily needs. Water was precious and its use had to be carefully conserved. The water was carried home in large water jugs. As was the custom, women carried heavy items on their heads. Yes, on their heads. Even a small person can carry substantial weight if it is properly balanced on the center top of the body. A cloth was wrapped in a circle to stabilize the weight on Antonetta's head. With help from neighbors the water-filled container was lifted onto her head. Allowing her hands to be free, she held onto her two small children for their walk home on those narrow uneven stone streets. This had to be done in every season of the year every day and in all weather conditions. Water for washing and bathing had to be heated in large pots on a grate in the fireplace. Everything involving the use of water required work.

    It is interesting to note that in Italy indoor plumbing was available to Romans thousands of years before but not for the villagers in the Southern Italian towns in the early twentieth century. Of course, without running water there were no toilets, just chamber pots which had to be emptied and cleaned daily. Mama was continually appreciative that in America she had the amazing convenience of a sink with a faucet delivering both hot and cold water on demand. No going to the well, no trudging home with small children and no heating water in large pots in the fireplace. And no chamber pots. God bless America!

Back to the button story. In Italy Mama was poor. Everything had a purpose and was valued. There were few shops in the village and women had to be self-sufficient. They wove cloth, sewed clothes, and knitted and crocheted shawls, sweaters, socks, blankets and hats along with making beautiful, embroidered household items. Also, there were no supermarkets as we know them, families kept chickens in their homes for eggs and the ultimate luxury of meat for a holiday meal.

One day Antonetta had put two buttons on the table to be used for a new dress she had just finished sewing for Grace, her baby girl. Well, the chicken saw the two pearly white objects and must have thought they were a delectable treat. One to be taken when no one was looking. But Mama was always on guard. As the chicken gobbled the two buttons, Mama grabbed the chicken and with the scissors she was just using to make the new dress, she slit its neck!

Angelo saw this and was just stunned. How could she sacrifice the chicken for just two small buttons? He was told to help hold the chicken and with the needle and thread that Mama had ready for sewing, Antonetta quickly stitched the chicken's neck with little loss of blood, but I am sure tremendous trauma to the chicken. Of course, the buttons were cleaned and then carefully sewn onto Grace's dress.

Angelo proudly recounted this as the first of his experiences as Mama's assistant in her future veterinary procedures in caring for the family's pets. He chuckled in reporting that the chicken lived on to produce many eggs and finally a delicious soup for a Christmas meal.

How poor and vulnerable she must have felt knowing that two buttons were of such value that she had to use whatever means in her power to retrieve them? And think of that chicken, she must also have been from sturdy stock to have survived her button snack and surgery!

As a child I would love to look in Mama's button box. It was full of all kinds of curiosities. Buttons made of wood, leather, pearl, cloth, bone and fancy diamonds (rhinestones). Big buttons and tiny satin buttons, buttons of all colors. These buttons must have been a small treasure for Antonetta who valued just two buttons for her baby's dress. Antonetta never discarded a button. When a garment was too old and worn it became a rag or used to wrap the fig tree in the backyard for winter. The buttons were always removed and added to Mama's collection.

After her death I inherited my mother's buttons. Whenever I need to replace a lost button, I know exactly where to find just the right color and size for the job. From time to time, I look through the box and think of its history. Each button has a story. Many years after Mama's death I am able to experience such a calming feeling by sifting through the buttons and holding something she held. I can feel the warmth of her spirit and have a strong connection to my family history. How amazing, mere recycled buttons can provide such a delicate thread to our precious past.

PADRE PIO AND THE BLACK DOG

In 1984 I was with my family on a vacation in Puglia, the Italian region of Italy. As we entered the Padre Pio Museum in San Giovanni Rotondo, I saw a large oil painting of the black dog. I lost all composure and started shouting "The black dog, the black dog!" My husband, Charles, son, Paul, and daughter, Meg, surrounded me and were shocked by my emotional outburst. They had heard my childhood story of the black dog but were not prepared for my reaction to this painting.

Padre Pio, Saint Pio of Pietrelcina was canonized a Saint in 2002 by the Catholic Church. What is this connection with the black dog?

In 1955 when I accompanied my mother to Italy, we visited many religious shrines. I was in awe witnessing Mama's fervor and deep concentration as we knelt, prayed and lit candles. At one site, we actually climbed an enormous stone staircase leading to the majestic church of Monte Maria Virgine on our knees! Many Italian Catholics believe this act of faith would save many years in Purgatory as one awaits transition to Heaven.

The absolute highlight of these spiritual visits was our pilgrimage to Padre Pio's Friday Mass. This Mass was the holiest of holies, for on this day his "wounds of Christ" bleed. Mass was celebrated in a small simple stone, candle-lit church in an impoverished town located in an almost hidden mountain valley in Puglia. San Giovanni is a neighboring village to San Marco in Lamis, the birthplace of my ancestors. Mama shared her days as a young woman attending not only Mass in San Giovanni but also her experience in the confessional with Padre Pio. She said "he knew us before we even said a word." His extraordinary spiritual connection to the villagers was taken with absolute seriousness. Padre Pio was often seen on long walks and graciously invited the villagers to join him in conversation and prayer. He was a friend as well as a spiritual force in their lives and he was remembered with affection and awe.

My mother and I traveled to San Giovanni on a Thursday night as guests of some distant relatives. This plan assured us proper arrival time at the church. We woke up at three a.m. to arrive at the church for the five o'clock Mass. Mama insisted on getting there early because it was a "must" for us to sit as close as possible to the altar. She always demanded a front row seat for everything. This was sure to be a spectacular religious "happening." That morning Padre Pio wore a simple white vestment and short white cloth gloves.

He bore the wounds of Christ – the stigmata on his hands and feet. They bled on Fridays because Jesus was crucified on Friday. Catholics believe that He died on the cross to take away the sins of the world. The faithful believed that Padre Pio was the living proof of this truth. To be close to Saint Pio was to be close to God in a special way. And we were in the very first row and saw the blood seeped through his gloves. It was also believed that he possessed the miraculous gift of bilocation. Thus, he could be in two locations at the same time and in different guises.

I remember a multitude of followers filling the church. They spoke many different languages, wore different types of clothing, and shared a diversity of olfactory treasures (fragrances, smells, and odors). Many had traveled great distances to be there that morning. In fact, I heard one family speaking Russian. In 1955 Italy this was quite unusual.

I was entranced by the many tall capuchin monks in their long brown robes with large wooden rosaries hanging from rope belts and wearing worn leather sandals. They were dressed in the garb of the Franciscan Order, founded by St. Francis, the first stigmatist. Their job, one they took seriously, was crowd control. They seemed mysterious and a little scary. The challenge was to accommodate the enormous crowd of pilgrims, many of whom made great sacrifices to travel there, to celebrate Mass with Padre Pio in his small country church.

Mass began and the many languages became one. In unison we all prayed in Latin. Incense was liberally spread from intricately sculptured containers on long silver chains. I became nauseous. The incense, the sight of the blood on the white gloves and the crush of human bodies of all sizes and ages overwhelmed me. I told my mother that I was about to vomit. "Oh, *Dio mio,* not at Padre Pio's Mass." What was I to do? There was such a crush of human bodies and no aisle for my escape. My mother told me to get down, crawl out and find my way back to the cousins' house. I did manage to squeeze my way through. Fortunately, the crowd was so engrossed and in full concentration of prayer that no one was at all distracted by this girl with two long braids weaving through their legs and over their feet.

Exiting the church, I took a gigantic breath enjoying the sweet mountain air. I had successfully made my way out of the church, but I had a major problem; I had no idea how to find the cousins' house. I did not know this town. We had just gotten there yesterday. I knew the house was located somewhere on the outskirts of the village but I did not remember how to find my way back.

As I stared out at the town, I saw a large gentle black dog sitting on the church steps. I love animals and the encounter with this beautiful beast was calming. We greeted each other and immediately became friends. He and I walked peacefully down the winding dirt road at a slow pace. I remember the tapestry of extraordinary colors in the early morning sky at sunrise. The grass seemed to have a special scent or was it the dog's breath? Pilgrims often spoke of the beautiful scent of flowers coming from Padre Pio's mouth as he spoke. We stopped. I looked up at the house and it did look familiar. My country guide, the black dog, patiently waited for me to be safely in the house.

Of course, none of the houses in San Giovanni were locked. In that town "Padre Pio protects everyone and everything." So, my mother was not at all concerned about sending me off on my own to find my way. Hours later when she returned and found me fast asleep Mama and the cousins were amazed. I told them how I met a black dog and he accompanied me along the road. I could not understand the excitement created by my walk with the black dog. What was this all about? Had Padre Pio bilocated in the guise of the black dog? Or perhaps his spirit entered the dog to guide me home. Whatever the explanation, Mama believed I was granted a miracle by the "Blessed Monk."

The story was repeated many times, to my father's family in San Marco, and when we returned home to our family and friends in New York. Sometimes I had to stand on a chair and tell all the *paesans*, friends, seated around the table every detail of the "miracle." At the time I was not at all convinced it was true and secretly believed this was an exaggerated leap of faith.

Padre Pio was not only a religious figure, but he also became a true hero to the people in that neglected area of Southern Italy. History documents the discrimination of the South by the North as Italy developed into an independent nation. So, it is easy to understand the significant needs of these Italians who were left behind.

In 1956 Padre Pio made an important decision. The donations he received from the many pilgrims visiting his church were to be dedicated to building a badly needed hospital. This was truly a blessing. There was no medical facility for the poor farmers of that region.

Today San Giovanni is a major tourist destination. There you will not only find the tomb of Saint Pio but also a world-class hospital. And I am proud to say our cousin Pasquale

Iantoschi, a doctor of internal medicine, is a member of its medical staff. When you visit today the little stone church is protected in a huge shrine where many can celebrate Mass on the grounds of Sant Pio's venerated burial place. He died on September 23,1968 and since then this date is designated Padre Pio Day throughout the Catholic world.

Seeing the oil painting of the black dog almost 30 years later shook me. Although my outburst seemed unsettling, I somehow had a feeling of centeredness in the memory of that walk with my furry guardian. Even now in the early morning when I am on the beach in East Hampton and see a fisherman with his black lab or when I recall the times I sat with Buddy, Nina and Nico's sweet black rescue dog, I remember my early encounter with Padre Pio's spirit. Gratefully, I am in harmony with a strong spiritual belief and the blessed gift of faith I was given as a child by my religious mother. Padre Pio is ever present in my prayers.

I wear the Padre Pio medal my cousin Grazia gave me to protect me in my illness. I wear this medal on a chain coupled with my mother's Madonna given to my daughter, Meg, before Mama died. Meg later lovingly gave the very same to me knowing how meaningful it was for me to wear it close to my heart. One Mother's Day, Meg also gifted me my very own Padre Pio stone statue for the garden. I enjoy seeing his smiling countenance in front of our little cottage and honor him with flowers in the spring and poinsettias at Christmas. Meg never tires of my Padre Pio stories and knows I am continually empowered by his healing prayer: *"Pray, hope and don't worry. God is merciful and will hear your prayer. Prayer is the best weapon we have; it is the key to God's heart."* Many believe through Padre Pio's intercession health can be restored. Perhaps it can – in this act of faith we will be blessed with strength and hope.

My dear family friend, Michael Tusiani, the son of Compare Michele continually nurtures our family ties and often sends me Padre Pio treasures from his travels. His bond and loyalty understand the spiritual strength Padre Pio inspires in my ongoing battle with cancer. His gracious wife, Bea's, my Comare, continued prayers to Padre Pio on my behalf cloaks me in the spirit of her love and the power of a positive outlook.

What I find so comforting is that my grandchildren also understand my attachment to Padre Pio and will bravely ask me questions about my religious faith. Especially Charlie, Paul's son. He and my daughter-in-law, Kate often invite me to go to Mass with them. Sometimes Isabel also joins us. Mama and I travelled a powerful spiritual journey together which has blessed me with a grounding forever present in my being.

Padre Pio in San Giovanni Rotondo, Italy 1950s

In 1929 Antonetta left her home and started a new life in America. Papa had come to the Bronx, one of New York City's five boroughs, in 1923 because of the Sammarchese community that had settled there establishing a support system for newly arrived immigrants. He found work thanks to a Jewish contractor who hired conscientious Italian workers ready for any job available. So, Papa settled in the Williamsbridge section of the Northeast Bronx.

At first, he lived in a boarding house, renting a room and saving money for six years until he found an apartment for his family. In 1929 Mama, Angelo and Grace arrived from Italy. The *paesans,* friends had a touching practice of helping newcomers by donating household items and furniture from their own homes, their own meager collections, to welcome the newly arrived families. They understood from their lived experience the needs of those who left their home countries with very little.

Life was transformed for Antonetta in America. She now lived in a three-room apartment with electricity, heat, running water and an indoor bathroom; what luxury! Papa was true to the promise he made to provide a better life for her and their children. Mama had to adapt to a very different environment. She learned to cook on a stove, use a washing machine instead of a washboard (which she always saved), shop in stores, use public transportation (buses and trains) and was able to send her two children to public schools. The family lived in two different apartments, one on East 215th Street and later on East 216th Street until they saved enough to purchase their own house on 220th Street. The neighborhood was kind of the same. The Bronx offered an established and diverse community with many resources. It was safe and friendly for the hardworking immigrants who took pride in their homes and raised their children with respect for others.

Antonetta was a walker. The family did not own a car. She was independent and did not want to depend on others for her needs. She shopped on White Plains Road which offered a variety of stores. She carried heavy bundles home until the reliable shopping cart became available. She bought 50 pounds of flour for her weekly bread making. These 50 pound cloth sacks were later recycled into all sorts of things such as sheets and household cloth items. At first, breadmaking began at home where she made the dough (flour, yeast, salt and water). She did not have an adequate oven in which to bake her bread. So, the kneaded dough was taken to the bakery. A service offered at the time to immigrants for a small fee. There it was baked in large ovens which were fired 24 hours a day.

Bread transportation was my brother Angelo's job. He dropped the kneaded dough off in the morning on his way to school and picked the beautifully baked crusty bread in the afternoon. Angelo was assigned this task when he first came to America. He was only eight years old. At Papa's direction he also had to build his own bread wagon. He was expected to find the materials himself! We had to become problem solvers. Papa was strict and set high standards for all his children. He was affectionately known as "Tough Tony" and we had the utmost respect for him. Papa was a war veteran, wounded in battle. He refused to have the bullet removed after he was injured in WWI fearing he might lose his leg. Although he walked with a slight limp, the bullet he carried from 1917 did not stop him from the strenuous work he did as a laborer (a plasterer). Nor did it limit him as a fearless hunter and passionate fisherman. He lived until the age of 81 after his final battle with lung cancer.

The owner of the bakery was interesting; Signora Angelina Martino, a widow, was also from San Marco and quite a character. She was a trailblazer; a successful woman owning her own business and becoming a money lender to many in the Italian community. I remember her coming to our house to visit Antonetta and enjoying a cup of coffee together. This was often done after she completed her serious banking at the stately Chase Manhattan Bank just up the street from our house on the corner of White Plains Road and 220th. At that time banking was always done in person. The two friends had so much to talk about. She called me "Dollie" when I was a little girl and when she hugged me, pressing me close to her ample breasts, I could hear the crunching sound of all the money she had stashed in her bra.

The Bronx offered Antonetta a neighborhood with friends who partied together on weekends. Among the good things they celebrated was their good fortune to be in America. They made music together (playing guitar and mandolin), they sang together, they feasted together, they were there for one another when times were bad and tragedy struck. They had the practice, *lu posta* (the place), contributing money when a person died to cover funeral expenses, especially the "place" to be buried. Early on most of the immigrants did not have life insurance to cover these expenses. This was a small but very supportive community from the same hometown in Italy with shared experiences.

I should mention Romano's Funeral Home also in the Bronx on White Plains Road as another *paesan* owned business. Old Mr. Romano was a kind man who tried to help his friends. He took care of all funeral arrangements knowing well the needs of those he served. He also had a fleet of limousines not only for funerals but available for weddings too. He was there to post bail and make contact with legal services serving as an interpreter for his community. Everyone knew Mr. Romano. After his death, his son carried on the spirit of service valued by the Sammarchese community.

Our location in the Bronx was close to the many beaches that line the Long Island Sound. One such beach was affectionately called "La Preta," The Rock. It was located in Pelham Bay Park and its lovely shade trees and sweet breezes offered a perfect picnic spot. In the summertime the *paesans* organized large picnics preparing delicious, cooked food and bringing gallons of homemade red wine. Everyone came ready for a good time. Women and children would try to sneak in for a quick swim but because this was an unprotected beach, with no lifeguard on duty, the mounted police sternly chased them all out of the water. The fun still continued with serious eating and drinking, music and card games. Laughter was always at a high volume. Life was good.

Mary Sassano, my sister Grace's godmother, was also a *paesan*. She was glamorous and flamboyant, always driving around in a brand-new Cadillac. Her devoted husband, Sapeen, was Papa's best friend. He took on second jobs just to keep his wife in beautiful cars and clothes. He saw the latest fashions on Fifth Avenue when he worked at construction sites in Manhattan and bought her lavish gifts. Her big, beautiful hats were her trademark. They had two children, Marylou and Michael.

Michael, their pampered first child, was drafted into the Korean War. Many heartaches followed. He was wounded and his life was never the same. However, when he was fighting in Korea, the frigid winter weather there ignited his mother's outrage. Her mother owned a knitting store on White Plains Road and Mary was an accomplished knitter. She knitted so fast that some reported sparks flying off her metal knitting needles. Mary designed and knitted Michael a khaki woolen face covering. But it did not seem fair to the other "boys" in his unit for only one guy to have this face protection. So, she bought tons of military green wool, made a pattern and established knitting circles which included most of the women she knew, to help knit these "helmets" as she named them. Antonetta immediately volunteered to host a circle and started knitting. Mary sent hundreds of knitted helmets to the American soldiers serving in Korea. Her efforts were even recognized in Washington, and she became a celebrity. She and her helmets made the front page of the New York City newspapers.

The Sammarchese men began a fun Sunday morning tradition by visiting the homes of their friends. They were all laborers who wore dusty, dirty work clothes during the week but not on Sunday. On this day they dressed up wearing three-piece suits and handsome Stetson hats; it had to be a Stetson! They came in as a group laughing and ready for exciting talk. Mama would quickly prepare the table in the upstairs kitchen with drinks, usually liquors she made herself, and of course, her homemade sweets she always had on hand to be served on these occasions. After the refreshments and conversation, they were ready for the next stop but before they left each child, "the little ones" was given a dollar bill and a big pinch on the cheek as their departing gift. In the 1940s a dollar really meant something; such a generous treat, one we remember well.

The Bronx also offered convenient public transportation. We had easy access to all of New York City since we did not own a car. The IRT subway line was a block away on 219th Street and White Plains Road offering an easy trip into Manhattan and to Bathgate Avenue. The trolley line also on White Plains Road was a quick ride to stores and movie theaters. Later the bus replaced the trolley, and this provided an easy ride throughout the Bronx to Fordham Road, the shopping mecca of the borough. The Bronx Zoo, City Island, and, of course, Orchard Beach were also within easy reach. The bus line also connected us to *paesans* outside the neighborhood. The Tusiani family, dear friends, required a bus trip to their house. I remember Compare Michele, my sister Provie's godfather, walking me and Mama to the bus stop after our visits. He was such a gentleman and a man of many talents. At Christmastime I would love to see the beautiful *presepio,* creche scene, he created himself. For Italians this honored tradition celebrating the birth of Christ brought a spiritual celebration and magic to the homes at the yuletide season.

The Bronx was welcoming to Italian immigrants but was also home to those of many from other ethnic and racial groups. We lived in a row of three attached houses, two of which were occupied by Black families whose children called our Papa, "grandpa." Mr. Johnson, who lived across the street, was our respected Black Fire Chief. Mrs. Marie MacDonald was a neighborhood favorite. She was an artist and opera singer who would often bring tea and home baked cookies out to her garden and invited us to join her among her beautiful flowers planted in memory of her "dear" husband, Mark. I remember her kindness and the interest she took in me as a young girl. We had Jewish, Irish, Italian, German and plain old American families that made up the wonderful people of 220th Street.

Antonetta loved the Bronx because its location offered her the freedom to navigate easily. She could walk to her children's schools, her parish church and all the funeral homes of choice. On Sunday afternoons she often visited the cemetery. Her beloved Woodlawn Cemetery is where Providenza (Provie), her daughter, who tragically died as a young mother, was buried. This was within walking distance from her home. However, it was a long walk that often resulted in Mama putting out her thumb and hitching a ride once she entered the cemetery gates. Of course, her children were shocked and counseled her not to do this, warning her of the dangers of getting into a stranger's car. She just shook her head and told us she had no fear because only good people would be visiting their dead in Woodlawn. Mama was right. There was never a problem.

When it came time to purchase her own cemetery plot she of course, chose Woodlawn. She checked all the available plots. After consulting her friends, Antonetta and Antonio Feltre decided to buy a plot together for three reasons. First, it would be larger, making a nice presence. Second, it was in the first row. This was extremely important to Antonetta since she insisted on being in front of everything. Third, it is located on Park Avenue, an important address for the laborers who worked throughout their lives on skyscraper construction projects in Manhattan. We were taught in real estate that the guiding principle was always location, location, location! Yes, the "Beautiful Bronx" was a dream come true for Antonetta.

Paesans Prank Papa
Top: Scivolone (mortician), Biangine (witness),
Sapeen (attorney), Del'Lueeg (priest),
Bottom: Vincenzo (advisor), Papa (stiff)
Bronx, NY 1940

Dr. Williams was our family physician. Antonetta's first encounter with modern medicine came after she immigrated to America in 1929. She met Dr. Williams when he began his practice at Fordham Hospital in the Bronx in 1930. Theirs was a special bond. He was at the beginning of his career, and she was being treated by a trained physician for the first time in her life. For those of us living in 2026, America needs some perspective to appreciate what this meant to an immigrant born in a different century and a different economic stratum.

Although the first medical schools were opened in the 9th Century Salerno in Southern Italy, medical care for the poor was not available to the common people. Mama's first encounter with modern medicine came after she immigrated to America. Doctors in San Marco treated the wealthy and served the important role of documenting deaths and their causes for all its inhabitants. There were no hospitals in that region until much later when Padre Pio built the first one to serve the agricultural communities of the small mountain villages in the provinces of Foggia.

In the early years women had their babies at home delivered by a midwife. Antonetta's first two children, Angelo and Grace were born in their one-room house during the cold winter months of December, for Grace, and January, for Angelo. Just think of the courage and strength of this young mother delivering her babies without her mother's support or any other women in her extended family. I remember the carefully preserved printed prayers Mama lovingly pressed into my hand before my son's birth, telling me that prayer was her strength when delivering her children.

In America delivering her babies at Fordham hospital with the care of an enthusiastic new doctor and support of real nurses was a blessing for Antonetta. She followed Dr.

Williams' care with ultimate respect and gratitude. She regarded him more than a professional. He was also a friend. She confided in him, and he confided in her, often receiving advice in dealing with the bossiness of his two sisters and the loneliness of his bachelor life.

When any family member was sick Dr. Williams was called, he came to our house ready to treat us. I remember Mama putting clean linen on the bed including the beautifully embroidered top sheet, the only one she brought with her from Italy. She felt privileged to have Dr. Willims in her life, dealing with all the illnesses that would have been fatal without the precious penicillin injection he always had handy in his black leather doctor's bag.

Dr. Williams was extraordinary in his service to the immigrant community. He made house calls even though he had regular office hours on the second floor of the home he shared with his two sisters on Barnes Avenue. He was always available to drive his patients for needed x-rays or laboratory procedures. He knew that many of his patients did not own a car and taxis were expensive. I remember Dr. Williams driving through the neighborhood and stopping his car if he saw us sitting on our cement "stoops" warning that sitting on cold cement was not good for our kidneys. He was always working on our behalf.

He had a mission to serve the immigrants in his community. He tended to their needs even when there was little they could give in payment. As the immigrant population changed from Italian to Latino to Haitian to Jamaican Dr. Williams continued to serve and remained in his community.

In documenting the contribution Dr. Williams made to our lives I tried to research his many years at Fordham Hospital. This was the first public hospital built in the Bronx in 1892 and closed in 1976. Fordham Hospital was demolished and is now the site of one of the Fordham University buildings. I could not locate medical records because I learned all public hospital records in New York City are destroyed after seven years.

Who was this man who devoted his life and talents to so many? Dr. Williams came up in the immigrant community and lived among the immigrants his whole life. He spoke Italian fluently and was sensitive to immigrant cultures and traditions. Some have said that he changed his name from the Italian, Guglielmo, to the anglicized, Williams to be more readily accepted into medical school when Italian candidates often faced discrimination. Few were admitted into the New York medical schools due to the prejudice against Italians during the 1920s and 1930s when he was being trained.

Although I did travel to the old neighborhood and found his house at 3664 Barnes Avenue, I could not find any record of his first name and never heard anyone, especially Antonetta mention it. I didn't ask and now I don't know. How easily a piece of history can be lost. Mama was not prone to hero worship, however, Antonetta's devotion to Dr. Williams lives on in our memories and powerfully in her prayers.

I was born in Fordham Hospital as were all my siblings born in America. It's ironic and sad that I don't know the real name of the man who assisted Mama with our births. Antonetta was content to call him "Dr. Williams." And so am I.

A short time ago I was reading Jo Piazza's book, *The Sicilian Inheritance* and it jarred my memory of my experiences with the *malocchio*. Dear reader, information explaining the *malocchio*, evil eye, is needed to fully appreciate its significance in this story. Italians and Italian Americans of Antonetta's generation believed in the power of folk magic to heal. If you knew the right rituals and prayers, you could dispel evil spirits. *Malocchio,* evil eye, was often cast (or so it was believed) by the jealous to bring down those whom they envied. In this belief systems, two things were vitally important: protection and cure.

The peasants of Southern Italy, especially the Sicilians, lived under conditions so harsh that we today can't even imagine their suffering. As food supply was insufficient, the average person lived an undernourished life. It's perhaps understandable that some would resent those who had a bit more than most and could wish them ill fortune.

Belief in one version or another of the evil eye goes back at least 5,000 years and is nearly universal. One could be cursed by a malevolent stare. But could also ward off its power by wearing the right amulets or reciting the right words. Many wore and still wear, little red horns (cornetto) around their necks in the belief it has the power to protect. What can one do in response to being cursed?

My brother Angelo was still serving in the navy after my birth, his wife Millie, separated from her husband, spent time with our family. As a young woman, recently married and without children of her own, she had a special relationship with me, the Lombardi baby. She loved to carry me in her arms, and her sweet affection is something I continue to remember even though I was only a toddler at the time.

One day we were sitting at the table with a group of *paesans* and as a curious toddler I grabbed a matchstick lying near a pack of cigarettes. I picked it up, pressed the match-stick into my mouth, sucking on it I swallowed the sulfur tip! Millie was also there that Sunday afternoon. Both Mama and Millie became upset. They tried, unsuccessfully to get me to spit up the sulfur tip. I remember the concern. I think I was given things to drink but nothing helped. I became nauseous and was told I had a change in skin color and exhibited some other reactions. I don't remember this too clearly because I was so young. What I do remember was Millie's emotional response. She was very protective of me and her concern tapped into her Sicilian superstitions that my "unusual beauty" elicited jealousy from someone at that table. Someone cast a curse and gave me the *malocchio*!

Antonetta was not a superstitious woman. For her magic came from the power of prayer. However, she was a practical person and was ready to try anything to make her *Teresina*, little Teresa, return to her rosy cheeks and robust health. Millie encouraged Mama to take me to see the *Vec-chia*, old woman in the community who had some secret powers. When Antonetta's attempts did not help her baby get better, she agreed. So, they packed me up and wheeled me in my rickety old carriage. The very one that serviced a long line of Lombardi babies. Off we went. I remember going to a dark apartment on the other side of White Plains Road. The woman was very old and wore a long dark dress. She was not scary, and I was not frightened. Introductions were made and Millie gave her version of what happened. Mama respectfully implored the old woman to help. The *Veccchia* brought a bowl or dish to the cloth-covered table and poured oil and water into the dish. There was some chanting or maybe praying. The room had no natural light and was lit by candles. I think I remember it getting very quiet. I am trying to recollect a childhood experience of more than 79 years ago. What is amazing is that although I don't recall most the details, I have strong memories (impressions really) of this experience. Why is this so vivid? Was it because I had never really seen Antonetta so worried and Millie so agitated? Was this a curse or a spell or a little child's physical reaction to the ingestion of sulfur? Whatever the explanation, I returned to my good health, and all was well.

Malocchio is a part of the immigrant experience. People wear red horns and gold horns, and we are taught the *mano fico,* index and pinkie finger gesture, in warding off bad luck. Sometimes new cars are even given red ribbons to tie around the inside steering wheel for protection from any possible bad luck. In our family usually a St. Christopher medal is given for blessings of safe driving from the patron saint of travel.

In my research I have found an Italian prayer to remove *Malocchio:*

Santa Maria, Madre di Dio, prega per noi peccatori adesso e nell'ora della nostra morte. Amen (English translation: O Mary, mother of God, pray for us sinners now and in the hour of our death.) This sounds very much like the Catholic Hail Mary prayer. Interesting. Women healers and a prayer to the Holy Mother.

Back to the story. In 1975 we lived in Brooklyn where my husband was serving a church on Ocean Avenue in Flatbush. My daughter, Meg was less than a year old and I enjoyed taking long walks with her sitting happily in her carriage looking beautiful in her white bonnet. We were walking along on Flatbush Avenue. There was a storefront where fortunes could be told for a fee, of course. The fortune teller came out of the shop and was trying to convince me to come inside to have my fortune told. I politely told her I was not interested. She kept trying and I kept saying "no" and I just continued walking. On my way back the fortune teller came out of her shop and confronted me again. She implored and I resisted.

She grew angry at my resistance. The more I resisted the angrier she got

Suddenly, she looked at Meg sitting in the carriage and gave her a most horrible glare. Yes, an evil stare. I was frightened. What could I do in response? Well, Millie had taught me. I looked straight into fortune teller's face, I did not say a word, I lifted my right hand and made the only gesture possible, the *mano fico*. I warded off her "curse" on my precious Babygirl. I took hold of the carriage handle never giving up the *mano fico* (with both hands) and walked all that way home knowing I had protected Meg from that evil woman! Once I got home, I felt safe. I could not believe that I resorted to such primitive behavior. Was this the "seamless blend of the magical and the real?" What else could I do? I had to be practical like Mama always was and used any means possible in this situation. I had to take action to form a dismissal of any possible evil doing. I did, and it felt so good!

Isabel, my firstborn grandchild has a way of tapping into family sensibilities. For her 23rd birthday she talked about wanting a small gold horn to wear on the chain I had given her with a medal of the Madonna and a small crucifix. My first stop was to the Macys jewelry department in the local Short Hills Mall. Their only offerings were very large sterling silver horns on heavy-duty chains. Not for our Isabel. I wanted to go to our local jeweler, Ferdinand's in New Providence, but I was embarrassed to request such an item because I didn't think Chris, who owns the store with her husband, Bill, would understand my intention with this gift. She is religious and we have sometimes shared prayers and Padre Pio stories. Not being Italian, Chris might not appreciate how the religious and superstitious can coexist in our spiritual world.

Charles and I knew exactly where we could find our gift. We traveled to the Bronx. To the Italian neighborhood on 187th Street. Sure, enough at Rocco's Jewelry Shop on the corner of 187th Street and Arthur Avenue we found the "real deal." Rocco has red and silver horns. He has all sizes of gold horns with or without diamonds! We found the perfect one for Isabel.

As I face my mature years, I am not at all self-conscious about these *malocchio* encounters. As Mama taught me, it is always best to have all bases covered, "for you never know!"

Millie & Theresa in The Bronx, NY 1945

The Italian immigrants shared important milestones with their *paesani*, friends. They were working class and had limited resources. They could not afford the extravagant catered weddings that we take for granted today. And so the 1940s and 1950s brought us the Football Wedding. It was an inclusive celebration where whole families, children, adults and of course, the elderly relatives who always had a place of honor, shared this joyous event in the lives of young couples. A reception hall was rented to accommodate the many invited guests.

An early tradition was for the couple to visit, and hand deliver the wedding invitation. Oh, what a thrill it was for us to host the wedding couple in our homes. This made possible a more intimate relationship with the bride and groom before the formal nuptials. They presented one invitation to each family and this invitation was taken to the reception on the day of the wedding as proof of inclusion. I guess this practice discouraged wedding crashers.

Antonetta was enthusiastic about attending these weddings. She took great care in dressing us up. Making a *bella figura*, good impression, as a family was important to her. She always believed that her children were the most beautiful and she put us on display with pride and joy. Mama made many of my clothes, especially my party dresses. These were usually made from organdy material that was starched and carefully ironed to create the most dramatic effect. She proudly wore her special navy-blue silk crepe dress with the elegant turquoise and silver beaded neckline. This, her one-and-only party dress.

The football wedding got its name from the unique distribution of the main refreshment served, sandwiches. Meat and cheese sandwiches, tightly wrapped in waxed paper were delivered to each table in a bushel that was emptied in the middle of the table for all to enjoy. The tight wrapping was a necessity since the sandwiches in crusty rolls were thrown through the air the length and width of the table at a person's request: a shout of "capicola and provolone" was answered with a toss like a missile into the outstretched arm of the thankful guest at the other end of the table. Thus the "football" title was born! These footballs were a treat and indeed delicious. There were always enough sandwiches to enjoy throughout the long night. I clearly remember my sister-in-law Millie, Angelo's wife, "reorganizing" the sandwiches after they were served. Her job was to make the sandwiches thicker by taking the meat and cheese out of some and adding it to others or by making meat only or cheese only choices. Of course, the empty rolls did not go to waste. They were brought home for breakfast the next day. I came to understand why women brought large purses to these parties.

The liquid refreshments were served in glass pitchers placed on each table. Orange soda for the children and beer and homemade wine for the adults. I loved the orange soda and when I reminisce, I can still taste that bubbly sweetness and the tell-tale orange mustaches on our young faces. My niece, Margo, reminded me of our joy in being able to drink as much of the refreshing orange drink as we could possibly consume was paradise. In the natural course of things our stomachs warned us when we had too much. Excess was the rule at the party. The dessert came later.

The music for these weddings was always provided by live bands playing a variety of musical favorites. What fun to see young couples dancing the jitterbug and the older folk the Italian tango. Children were always welcomed on the dance floor. My favorite was an Italian folk dance, the *Tarantella*, not only because it was an intergenerational dance but especially because Antonetta came forward with her father's wooden castanets, and her friend, Comare

Archangelina, played her old, worn but very faithful tambourine. These instruments were one of the few treasures they brought with them from Italy to America. I remember how serious Antonetta was as she placed her fingers in the leather strips beginning the clackety-clack dancing with her hands held up in joyous revelry. What was she remembering? For us the lively music and the ancient folk-dance steps were so much fun. One could feel the old-world connection as all cheered on the final note. A part of their past was very much present from San Marco to the celebration of their enriched lives in America.

At this point in the party the Busta Line began at the table of the wedding couple. The *busta,* envelope was the gift that each family in attendance gave to the newlyweds. In our tradition the wedding gift was always cash. The money helped the newly married couple to begin their life together. The envelope was given to the couple and was carefully placed into a busta bag, a white satin drawstring sack usually trimmed with beautiful lace that held the precious gifts.

As a thank you the bride and groom reciprocated with a little gift for the guests. This was called the "favor." Usually, the favor was a small pottery or metal memento holding a white net pouch of sugared almonds tied with a white ribbon stamped with the names of the happy couple. When visiting the homes of the *paesani* I would love to see special shelves dedicated to the display of the many wedding favors received through the years. Antonetta kept her collection of favors in a credenza in the living room. These were displayed along with the exotic blue china my brother, Lou, brought back for her from Japan, one of the many countries he visited while serving in the U.S. Navy during the Korean War.

Next, the special music of the Grand March signaled the beginning of this ceremonial parade by everyone in the hall. The bride and groom led their families and guests as they pranced around the hall in time to the ceremonial music. The women in their beautiful dresses and the men in the one suit they owned, participated in a moment of celebration and elegance. Of course, the children were always included in this festive procession.

At last it was time for dessert, time for the sweet treats. The bride and groom culminated the activities by carrying a huge tray of cookies and cream puffs to each table to personally serve desserts to their guests and thanking them for their gracious *auguri,* wishes. The sweets were often homemade by members of the bride or groom's family.

I remember hearing a story told by my brother Angelo about his wedding in 1944. Antonetta asked some close friends from Long Island City to guard the tray of treats before the reception while everyone was at the church. Well, these friends could not resist the delicious, sugar-coated cookies Mama had made. They decided to sample a few and then a few more, seriously diminishing nearly half the tray. With each telling of this story everyone laughed and Long Island City continues to have a bad rep!

My nostalgic memories of these football weddings of the past fill me with thoughts of all the characters in our Sammarchese community who enhanced my life. And especially the joy Antonetta expressed at seeing her friends and family sharing in these happy moments together. However, as times changed and we became more affluent the football wedding became a "thing of the past." Our once intergenerational celebrations have become exclusively adult as the high cost of the modern wedding has limited the guest list. We rarely see children sliding across the dance floor and guzzling orange soda. Also, as a sign of our economic progress, wedding invitations are no longer delivered personally because we no longer live in close ethnic communities. Often live music is replaced with DJs. Sadly, the Grand March is no more. The *Tarantella* is rarely danced at weddings today and the haunting melodies to which we danced it have been eliminated from the song list. The Busta Line is gone but the tradition of the wedding money gift continues on. Definitely a good move. Oh, how I miss the fun of football weddings. I cannot think of them without remembering Mama, her joy playing her father's castanets.

Antonetta's Father's Castanets
Handmade in Italy, early 1900s

MORE THAN FRIENDS
THE LOMBARDI AND THE TUSIANI FAMILY

For many immigrants coming to America and their departure from Italy was a wrenching separation. They left family, culture, environment and the past behind in the hope of a new life in the "the land of milk and honey." Antonio and Antonetta began a new life in a new land without any relatives of their own. As a child growing up I was very much aware of the absence of aunts, uncles, and cousins in my life. My living aunts, uncles and cousins lived thousands of miles away and across a large ocean. I only knew them through the letters and pictures we received as a result of Antonetta's dedicated correspondence throughout the years.

In the Italian community the honored role of godparents joined us to other families forming a bond that was more than friendship. Michele Tusiani, Compare Michele, was my sister Provie's godfather. She was Antonetta's first surviving child born in America in 1933. He joined our extended family early. Our strengthened relationship began when he was alone in this country while his wife, Comare Maria, and their scholarly son, Joseph, were still in San Marco awaiting migration. The relationship was strong and lasting.

Provie's godfather was an interesting and talented adult in our lives. Compare Michele was a playwright, actor, musician and artist and as I fondly remember, a perfect manner. He was a gentleman. Each Christmas we were dazzled by his *presepio,* creche spectacular. He created a religious wonderland in his home displaying Christian figurines and scenes he sculpted and painted himself. As a child a visit to the Tusiani house made Christmas real.

His beautiful wife, Comare Maria, and Antonetta were good friends in San Marco as single women and later as young mothers. Upon her arrival to America in 1947 Mama embraced this friendship anew and they spent time together especially after the birth of her second son, Michael, who has become an honorary brother in the Lombardi family. He and his wife are always seated with the brothers and sisters at any Lombardi family event, and he has nurtured us with his extraordinary generosity. After the deaths of our parents, we became orphans together. His affectionate wife, Bea, and their children seamlessly joined our family. We celebrated joyfully and mourned tenderly together throughout the years.

Joseph Tusiani, the highly educated and accomplished first son became a source of pride for the whole Sammarchese community in the Bronx. These *paesans* had little or no formal education. They were mainly homemakers and laborers. I remember Joseph's visits to my home. My father, as a sign of respect for Joseph's learning, would suddenly start speaking formal Italian, the language very different from the dialect spoken with family and friends. Joseph, who was referred to as *"professore"* by my parents, was born and educated in Italy, published many books, received international recognition for his poetry and literary works in four different languages and secured positions in American universities. Outstanding accomplishments for a son of San Marco. He is a superstar in our immigrant community and beyond.

Last year one of Joseph's poems was selected by William Healy, my sister, Provie's gifted grandson, for a work he composed for a city-wide competition on life in New York. William's mother was only 15 months old when her mother, Provie, died.

Many years ago, in their young adult lives Provie and Joseph knew each other and shared a mutual interest in Emily Dickenson's poetry. Carey's son did not know his grandmother. What a meaningful connection to the past. William's composition was a link to his grandmother, Joseph's poetry and the work of Emily Dickenson. This was certainly an interesting connection: a grandson's music, a long dead grandmother's poetical interest and her godfather's son's poetry, all brought together in a young composer's original work: *New York Revisited.* Amazing!

Michael Tusiani, the second son, was born in New York in 1948. He became a noted business leader in both this country and abroad. He also is a published author. Michael's generosity to family and friends is legendary. He and his wife have been unfailingly gracious to the Lombardi family and many others in their circle of friends. Their generosity and support have enriched many lives.

Recently, Michael and his wife, Bea, hosted a group on a six-day trip back to San Marco to dedicate a sculpted bench and statue in honor of Joseph, the celebrated son of San Marco. An enthusiastic crowd included many from this Pugliese village as well as scholars, civic leaders, musicians, an American contingent and even the Italian RAI television station. What I found most thrilling was the display of genuine affection of so many for an intellectual and academic giant. Michael and his family included me, my husband, my brother, and his wife, in this family milestone which extended to days of exploration and enjoyment of our Italian roots in the Pugliese countryside. We enjoyed sightseeing tours, sumptuous meals and Easter Week religious celebrations.

On our visit to the shrine of San Michele, reenacting a ritual I remembered from my childhood visit in 1955, Bea and I were joined as godmothers. We dipped our fingers into the sacred font, shared a prayer and exchanged a kiss, forever connecting us as true *comare* for yet another generation. A bond deeply religious and truly emotional. A highlight of my trip.

Unfortunately, we have had to share unbelievable sadness as adopted families. The passing of our parents and siblings and the tragic deaths of the young: Pamela and Catherine Tusiani, our sister, Provie, great niece Michele Chebetar, and nieces Susan and Carol Ann Lombardi. We share feelings of the rejection of fate and personally question life's meaning. Antonetta and Comare Maria were armed with a deep faith and a grounding in their Catholic religion. And although they had to withstand the economic *miseria* in Italy, ours is of a more spiritual nature.

We see the devastation in the youth of our society today and the difficulty in finding meaning and contentment. And with the demolition of the nuclear family, the once powerful shield so dominant in providing an emotionally protective barrier to confusion is now being seriously eroded. But we are fortunate to have experienced the unconditional love of parents and siblings. And that love has enabled us to seek the higher good.

I am grateful to see this spirit in my grandchildren and to have encountered it in Michael Tusiani-Eng, Paula and Roger's younger son and Bea and Michael's 17-year-old grandson. On our trip to San Marco he was unfailingly kind, helpful, and supportive of the somewhat "challenged" adults in the group. In making connections we nurture the relationships that help us face life's pain and disappointment.

Gratefully, the bond of the Lombardis and the Tusianis has only deepened and strengthened with time. Our families, more than friends, continue to share pain and celebrate together. Our relationship inspires in us the courage demanded as we continue on life's journey. Fortunately, Antonetta's and Comare Maria's lessons still guide us.

Three Generations of Tusianis
Top: Paula, Michael. Bottom: Bea, Michael, Sculpture of Joseph
San Marco in Lamis, Italy 2024.

Mama had two kitchens: an upstairs kitchen and a down-stairs kitchen. The Lombardi house was a modest two-family attached home in a working-class section of the Northeast Bronx. Antonetta was always grateful that she was able to own her house. She loved her house and often said that it had all the "conveniences" she needed.

The second floor contained a rental apartment that helped to pay the many expenses faced in home ownership. In the 1940's my sister Grace moved home from Cincinnati with her husband Bill and their two children, Billy A and Margo. They lived upstairs until they could buy their own charming house just one block away on 221st Street.

The first-floor apartment was where Mama and Papa lived with their unmarried children. This "railroad" dwelling had three bedrooms, a living room, one bathroom, a kitchen and a *stanzina*, a tiny room for Mama's Singer sewing machine. Antonetta bought this machine "on time" during the depression for an exorbitant price. She knew this investment would "pay off" since it enabled her to sew the many items she completed as piecework common to the at-home female workforce of that time. That Singer sewing machine has a place of pride in my home and is still in use today.

The small sunny porch off the kitchen was the location of the essential clothesline overlooking our patch of green. This outdoor space provided room for all sorts of Lombardi happenings: from an outdoor reception for Provie and Bob's wedding, to a garden complete with a large fig tree that was dutiful covered every winter, a fragrant peony bush, beau-tiful roses that bloomed in May (honoring the Madonna) and of course, outdoor barbeque grills.

Below the first floor was the cellar. Not just any ordinary cellar. For me, this was a wonderland. There was a street en-trance and a small room that once served the coal chute which evolved into other uses and finally became my little study. The cellar had a huge kitchen, which included a wringer washing machine, an upright piano and a seating area with a couch. A serious table that could serve at least 20 guests and a huge sink and "wash tub." A small bathroom led to another room. This adjoining room contained Papa's wine making equipment as well as an adequate supply of wine and of course, the small vinegar barrel. On top shelves Mama stored canned tomatoes and hanging across the space was a line for preparing cured meat strips.

Lastly, the boiler room housed a huge coal-converter boiler which provided just the right temperature for drying laundry. The warm space also enabled yeast to do its magic when combined with water, salt and flour for Mama's crusty homemade bread and pizza. The dough was kneaded on a wooden table that could be disassembled and turned into an efficient portable workstation that was easily stored.

Back to the two kitchens. Mama's upstairs kitchen was reserved for light cooking, breakfast, coffee, liquors and homemade sweets served to guests plus the nightly family meal that was cooked in the downstairs kitchen and brought upstairs for the family to enjoy without seeing all the mess involved in its preparation. Breakfast included juice from one freshly squeezed orange for each child, oatmeal, farina, biscotti or cornflakes. The children then lined up for the daily dose of cod liver oil given from the largest spoon Mama had reserved in her spoon collection for this medicinal practice. We then sat down and enjoyed a steaming cup of *latte caffe*, mostly heated milk and a small amount of espresso coffee remaining in the pot left by Papa before he went to work. On very cold mornings just before leaving the house, Mama had a warming morsel for us making our walk to school more bearable: one delicious cherry marinated in pure grain alcohol that she lovingly popped into our mouths! I wonder what the teachers would have thought if they knew of this frigid morning Lombardi practice.

The second kitchen, the cellar kitchen, the work kitchen, was a serious workshop. In the center of the space was an oversized wooden table that served as a workstation for all the labor-intensive foods Antonetta prepared, and was easily converted into a gracious dining table large enough for all her children and grandchildren, and on special occasions it was used for parties for our *amici,* friends. The table was carefully set with chipped china, mismatched silverware and recycled jelly glasses for beverages. Although the dough for fresh pasta was made on the board in the boiler room, this table provided the needed surface for the celebrated pasta machine to roll out strips to be filled with a ricotta mixture for ravioli served on holidays, also linguini paired with special sauces and of course, the star of the show, the *crustales*, the Christmas *Sanmarchese* sculptured honey treat our family still makes today. I was fortunate to have inherited Antonetta's URANIA pasta machine. Each year I bring out Mama's classic recipe and her pasta machine to carry on a tradition with Antonetta's granddaughter, Meg and great grandchildren, Nico, Nina, and Paul's children, Isabel, Maisy, and Charlie as a gift lovingly presented to the Lombardi family and friends. You should see our youngest granddaughter, Nina, cranking out the dough. She is the master of the pasta machine!

The cellar table was also the workspace for assembling the year's supply of bottled tomatoes, tomato sauce and tomato paste. These were carefully canned for use throughout the year. At summer's end when tomatoes were most ripe and delicious, the mass production of cutting tomatoes and filling Mama's collection of recycled soda bottles, with basil and salt and to be pushed snugly in with wooden dowels began. Everyone in the family was recruited for this project. However, there was one serious rule: if a female member had her period she could not participate because of an old belief that this would cause the bottles to explode! I doubt there is scientific evidence to support this theory.

Antonetta only served food made from the most pure and fresh ingredients, never canned or frozen foods. She often dressed live chickens, rabbits and ducks which she raised herself in our backyard and even pigeons purchased at a local pet shop for Papa's favorite sauce. My sister Nan loved to share the memory of her extreme embarrassment as a child having to go to the pet shop on White Plains Road to buy this unique ingredient for Sunday dinner. The pet shop owner would ask if pigeons were "for cooking or pets." He was very well aware of the immigrant practices in his neighborhood. Nan quickly walked home carrying the brown bag with poked air holes keeping the pigeons alive. They had to be fresh, maintaining Mama's strict standard for quality control. I have a more pleasant memory of watching Mama sitting at that table and stripping lamb bones and curing the meat strips with red pepper, salt and fennel seeds which were then hung to dry and later roasted or grilled to perfection. It was a treat I loved. Angelo, a great storyteller, would recite his tale of cowboys roasting dried meat over campfires out on the range. As a child, I wondered if these cowboys were also from San Marco.

For a delicious protein Mama prepared different types of fish which Papa, an avid fisherman, proudly brought home from his many fishing excursions at City Island. Papa brought home live eels caught in the swampy canal in Cos Cobb, Connecticut. He promptly put his catch into our bathtub. Oh I remember showing my friends the long black eels, looking more like long black snakes swimming in the water. This was quite a sight! Of course, the eels had to be fresh before they were grilled as a special family treat.

Brother George, an avid fisherman himself, was often Papa's fishing partner and inherited his love for fishing, catching larger and more challenging fish from the Long Island coastal waters and the deep Atlantic Ocean every year since.

Each fall brought a unique kind of food preparation to our cellar – wine making! Many 25-pound crates of California grapes were delivered to our basement by Angelo, the fruit merchant on White Plains Road. Red grapes and white grapes. As a little boy of three or four our son, Paul, who loved grapes could not believe his eyes when he saw this volume of his favorite fruit. He immediately jumped on a pile face first to eat up as many grapes he could fit in his mouth. We all laughed and tucked away another memory of a fun experience in the cellar kitchen.

Papa carefully washed several oak barrels in preparation for the winemaking. The heavy-duty crusher was placed on top of the dry, open barrels for the process of crushing the grapes. Brother Angelo, our resident engineer, often had to repair the electric mechanism on this old crusher for its smooth operation. Squeezing the grapes allowed the juice and the yeast on the skins to combine for fermentation. When the chemical process was ready, the liquid was pressed and transferred to smaller barrels for aging, waiting for just the right time to be siphoned into bottles. Each year and each crop brought a different taste. Sometimes great, sometimes good and sometimes okay but always drunk at mealtime, at happy celebrations and to assuage painful sadness. It was often given as gifts for a taste of the old world.

Antonetta was thankful for the *abbondanza*, the abundance, her downstairs kitchen stored. I often think of how courageous these immigrants were. They left their home country, escaping *la miseria*, the poverty that was truly life threatening. In particular, Southern Italians were malnourished and many, especially those who lived in cities, died of starvation. They came to America so that their families could survive and prosper. They never forgot those painful years

they left behind and became loyal Americans who were forever proud and grateful of their new country.

Millie, Mama, Theresa, Grace with
Paesan Women in Downstairs Kitchen
Bronx, NY 1955.

Mama always had pets. Our pets were part of the family and had their jobs like the rest of us. They were loved and their roles were respected. After all they were animals. Cats caught mice and dogs were our security system. They ate the same food that we ate. There was no such thing as store bought pet food in our house. We often had both a dog and cat, as well as chicks and rabbits that joined the family at Eastertime. Our house on 220th street was an attached house with a front and back porch and an adequate back yard to meet an immigrant family's cultural seasonal practices. A long cool alleyway connected the yard to the basement. Each year Mama white-washed that alley with a homemade broom made of corn husks. Nothing went to waste and many things that were needed were made by hand. Mama was definitely one of the most self-sufficient people ever. The space under the porch was a functional storage site as well as a rain protected area for all sorts of activities.

Getting back to our pets, this is a dog story amusingly told by our brother, Angelo, and sister Nan. Mickey, the dog, was having some kind of an intestinal issue. Our pets were not sent to the veterinarian. Mama was the vet in our house. One of her most reliable cures was cod liver oil, which she also gave to her children each morning. Unfortunately, Mickey may have had worms and did not respond to the cod liver oil therapy, so Mama progressed to a more serious treatment. Since he was a young dog, she decided it must be a case of worms, and the only cure was to cut his long tail. Mama loved animals and felt a bond to every living creature. She could not bear to see an animal suffer and was always ready to help.

The operating theater for this surgery was the space under the back porch. This space was an efficiently organized small space containing yard equipment, and a small table with an enameled tabletop that could be easily cleaned and sterilized. Mickey was tied to a post and placed on the table. The first step was to carefully clean his tail with Mama's anesthetic, the 190-proof grain alcohol she also used to make anisette and other liquors. Next with her handy large cleaver and one strong stroke chopped off Mickey's tail. With a piercing yelp the job was done. She dressed the wound with iodine and a large white bandage made from strips of fabric that had a previous life as an article of clothing. Mickey looked at Mama and she held Mickey with warmth and affection, cooing a gentle song. Mickey survived the surgery and lived a long and healthy life.

My sister, Nan, loved adding to the story by telling how she picked up the tail and proudly showed it to all her friends in the neighborhood. This was yet another example of how they were awed by the unusual activities of our Italian mother. Not everyone in the Bronx had a mother who was also a veterinarian.

On my trip to Italy with Mama in 1955 I remembered our ship docking in Naples. It brings back memories of coffee and its connection to my mother. We had some time to spend in this port city before our train ride to Foggia, the nearest city to our beloved San Marco in Lamis. Mama and I were walking, walking, walking. The crowd of gregarious Neapolitans offered a fascinating appeal to a ten-year old American girl visiting Italy for the first time. I was experiencing a different culture yet one that was surprisingly familiar. There was an animated spirit, yet a profound sadness in these people. A sadness so present after the Italian experiences of WWII. All around us were remnants of Italy's painful defeat. Although it was ten years after the end of the war, we saw evidence of the brutal destruction, the collapsed buildings, the bullet holes in stone walls, the maimed war veterans and the many poor people wearing tattered clothing.

Mama knew we needed a coffee boost. After all, we were in Naples. She found an outdoor coffee cafe – bar and marched us up to the counter joining the men. Yes, mostly men, wearing their tailored suits crisp but new in a previous time. They wore jackets casually draped over their shoulders and worn leather briefcases under one arm. This was not a style seen at home in the Bronx. A coffee and *sfogliatelle* were ordered for each of us. *Sfogliatelle* is a delicate Italian pastry (which I later learned is the symbol of Naples). This spun shell-shaped sweet, stuffed with a custard-like filling and pieces of sugared fruit offered a delicate crunch and subtle sweetness with every scrumptious bite.

My life changing coffee experience was about to begin. I watched in amazement as this giant copper and brass coffee maker sputtered and hissed its coffee like a magic genie. Mama stirred in three small lumps of sugar and with a smile said *bere*, drink. The steaming aroma from that chunky little cup, with no milk and the sweet smell of the warm *sfogliatelle* partnered to form a precious experience I can still smell and taste these many years later.

What were Mama's thoughts as we stood there drinking coffee? Was she remembering the day she embarked on that giant ship transporting her to a new life? Was she imagining how she was going to rejoin her husband and begin their marriage again after a long separation in a different time and different place? Was she dreaming about the wonderful opportunities for her family in New York, in *l'America*, the land of opportunity. Poor Italian immigrants were eager to come to America. Their adopted country offered food, it offered warmth and safety, most of all it offered hope.

Espresso coffee, an Italian ritual, was a part of our lives across the Atlantic Ocean into our sunny kitchen in the Bronx. As children, coffee was part of the morning breakfast along with a glass of one freshly squeezed orange and biscotti or corn flakes. Ours was not the black coffee of the adults but our own half milk and half coffee, *latte e caffe*. And of course, sugar was added to cut the bitterness of the strong coffee and to give us the energy we would need for our long walk to school. Mama used freshly ground coffee beans. When I was old enough, my job was to go "up the avenue" to buy the coffee at what seemed to me, a mysterious coffee store. The shop was one block up the street on White Plains Road. Many ethnic stores lined the street in our diverse neighborhood in the Williamsbridge section of the Bronx. The coffee store was owned by a robust German gentleman. He was a large man who smiled easily and wore a gray apron with huge pockets. Although I can't remember his name, I can still see his face so clearly as he helped customers and worked side by side with his patient wife. This was a chore I loved. Just entering the shop and hearing the bell ring overhead as I entered drew me into an amazing sensory fantasyland. Large bags of coffee with names of different countries stamped on the burlap bags lined on one side of the aisle and bags full of grains and nuts sat on the other. How did these beans make their journey to this shop?

Upon entering my senses were immediately bombarded. The store was old and dark, having worn, wide-planked wooden floors and a monstrous black cash register that looked like it weighed at least half a ton. There was also this wonderful red metal coffee grinder on the counter ready to transform the beans into just the right texture for each type of coffee pot, perk pots, drip pots and Italian espresso coffee makers. I would take my time while a customer requested their beans ground. Oh, what a treat just to smell the aroma of the freshly ground coffee beans. It immediately took me back to the coffee bar in Naples – the coffee and the *sfogliatelle*.

I knew my mother was waiting for me at home, confident in knowing that I could complete my little task in a neighborhood that was safe, one where adults "looked out" for children. Memories are our connections. I often wonder how my mother was so nurturing when she herself was deprived of the love of her parents at such an early age. How did she survive as an orphan at nine years old without a family? The Naples coffee encounter is one of the many precious moments I shared with the tiny woman who encouraged me to reach out, to be unafraid, to be courageous in facing life's challenges and enjoy its amazing possibilities.

Orchard Beach, known by some as the "The Riviera Of New York City," was a bus ride away from our house on 220th Street in the Bronx. This city park encompasses some 115 acres, the brainchild of Robert Moses, New York's then urban planner and provides a summer getaway for thousands of Bronxites. According to the official record, "The sand was brought by barge from Sandy Hook New Jersey and Rockaway in Queens." The crescent shaped man-made beach includes a handsome promenade with a mile long walkway and sweeping views of City Island. The beach is surrounded by acres of "natural forest, marshlands and coastline" providing shady picnic areas for all to enjoy. The well planned and carefully designed bus depo makes for easy access and efficient passenger connections. With clear signage and individual bus stations, one could transition from a lazy beach experience to the trip back to a Bronx neighborhood easily. Orchard Beach opened in 1936 and continues as a popular "hot spot" on the Long Island Sound

For both Mama and Papa growing up in San Marco offered beautiful mountain-top views of Italy's Gargano coast along the Adriatic Sea. They were instilled with an attachment to the beach with all its gifts and grandeur. Papa was a lifelong passionate fisherman, a genetic thread woven through the lives of his three sons, Angelo, Lou and George and continuing to his grandsons, especially Marco, Nan's son.

Mama, on the other hand, was the beachcomber. She loved the magic of the sand and sea. At the seashore she found beauty and a sense of calm in her busy life. Burying her hands, legs and feet in the hot sand was Antonetta's heat therapy for the aches of arthritis. And the saltwater baths were an essential medicinal cure for ailments suffered by adults and little ones. She always advised us on the body's need for salt water.

One of the many "conveniences" of living in the northeast Bronx was having Orchard Beach within easy traveling distance for lunch and an afternoon dip. We were able to travel to this gem of a city park by taking two buses. One on White Plains Road to Pelham Parkway and then a transfer (at no cost) to the Orchard Beach Line. Antonetta would coordinate these beach trips with her dear friend Comare Maria Tusiani and Michael, her son, Margo and Billy A, my sister Grace's children for whom my mother often babysat and me, who always happily joined the beach adventure. My niece Margo remembers how Mama performed her *ficca nanza,* the Italian behavior of not wanting to wait in a long line and maneuvering herself to the front often at the dismay of others. She simply looked forward and pushed the children ahead. An embarrassing moment for us but not for Antonetta.

An afternoon's frolic at Orchard Beach demanded serious planning. First a telephone call to Comare Maria confirming the meeting place along the bus route. Once on route their connection was made by shouting to each other through the bus windows, in Italian, of course, at the rendezvous point. A true embarrassment for the children.

Upon arrival and set up of our beach blankets lunch was served. Lunch was always some wonderful combination of leftovers; broccoli rabe, chicken, fried peppers and or cheese, between two thick slices of Antonetta's crusty homemade bread. The sandwiches were wrapped in wax paper and placed in brown paper bags that usually leaked the tell-tale signs of extra virgin olive oil, a must for a tasty sandwich. The beverage served in recycled glass soda bottles was Papa's homemade wine mixed with ginger ale enjoyed by adults and children alike. Dessert was always a piece of juicy in-season fruit carefully selected for its peak flavor. We had to wait at least twenty minutes before our plunge into the sound. We were warned that this time was needed to digest our food and to prevent a cramp while swimming which would surely cause us to drown.

Beach bathing required several steps. First, a bathing suit was worn under our clothes for a quick change to ready us for our aquatic frolicking. Then the delicious plunge into the water. This was mandatory at every age whether we were ready or not, bobbing up and down with the necessary soaking of the body's bottom. This, Mama believed, was an important health benefit for the body's well-being. The last step of our bathing adventure was most painful and distressing for the children. Removing the wet bathing suit and changing into dry clothes was a must for any self-respecting person of European heritage. The Americans around us did not share this view and, of course, we were horrified at what they would think of us. Mama would wrap herself in a big towel and wiggle out of her suit, putting her cotton dress over her head and pulling it down over her body. She then sat down and discreetly unraveled her panties, or "bloomers" as she called them, and rolled them on completing the challenging task. Now she was ready to soak up the sun and to enjoy the warmth of the hot beach.

I clearly remember the embarrassment of the changing ordeal. No one else on the beach participated in this practice. However, I also remember the comfort of the dry cotton on my skin and the ease with which the whole devastating changing act was quickly forgotten when Mama pulled out her little black change purse. This signaled our beach treat. Coins for ice cream at the concession stand jingled and we jumped to the sound and were ready to make our way up for the creamy, cool taste of summertime.

At the appointed hour Mama and Comare Maria packed everything up and prepared for our trip home. Yes, they had to return in time to prepare the evening meal for their husbands and families. I fondly remember that wondrous time on Orchard Beach with Mama and our Sammarchese beach buddies, Comare Maria and her engaging little son Michael.

Antonetta, Margo & Mrs. Panitieri
Orchard Beach, Bronx, NY 1950s

All of Antonetta's children attended Public School 13 in the Bronx. Mama and Papa were well known because of the many children who attended the traditional two-story red brick building on East 216 Street. Their neighborhood school was about a 15-minute walk from home. This school was built in 1888 designed with the building's entrance having two separate external staircases: one for girls and one for boys. Girls wore dresses or skirts, and the boys were given no opportunity to sneak peeks when they climbed the stairs entering the classrooms.

Unfortunately, this sturdy old building that served the community for so long was demolished. The school principal was Miss Bjorklund. She was there when my oldest brother Angelo started school as a newly arrived Italian immigrant in 1929 and continued as the educational leader until the youngest Lombardi, Theresa, graduated from sixth grade in 1956.

Antonetta and Miss Bjorklund had a unique relationship. Mama would tell her how "youngle" (young) she looked, a welcomed compliment and she would tell Mama that hers were the most beautiful children in the school. A fact that Antonetta believed all too well. Theirs was a "mutual admiration society." Although Antonetta was older than the other mothers when I was a student and her style, was certainly different from theirs; she was comfortable in that educational institution and felt welcomed by the principal. And to think she herself had only gone to the third grade!

Miss Bjorklund supervised a loyal group of all female teachers. Many of whom were either Irish or Jewish serving a diverse student population. Although my parents had limited English proficiency, they had no trouble reading and understanding our report cards. This they did faithfully. The grading system was straightforward and easy for all students and families to understand. The grading: *A, B, C, D, or F* were clear performance standards. For us *A* was the expected grade. Anything lower was a disappointment. Papa was strict and Mama simply expected the best from us.

The standard of excellence was actually set by my sister Provie who was the academic star of the family at P.S. 13 and later at Evander Childs High School where her name is present on the school plaque in the front lobby as an outstanding student. I remember beginning each school year and being referred to by the teachers as "Providenza's little sister."

For most immigrants, free public education was highly valued. Free public-school education in the Italy of my parents' time was only available until the third grade. Their disappointment in not having more classroom instruction was obvious to us throughout their lives. For their children having an education was of utmost importance and we were constantly reminded of it being key to a successful future. Papa worked as a laborer doing backbreaking jobs with no security. He kept a little shovel in the corner of the kitchen as a reminder of what life without an education had in store for us.

We were lucky to live in New York City because it offered free public education from elementary school through to college. An opportunity cherished by many immigrants. City College was one of the schools in the city university system which I was fortunate to attend. City College was called the "Proletariat Harvard" due to its high standards and having many recognized leaders in all fields on its roster of graduates.

Antonetta faithfully attended all school functions. Miss Bjorklund was appreciative and sought her out each time. I remember that she gave Mama a complimentary ticket for a school show during the Korean War when my brother Lou was home on leave from the Navy. Mama proudly attended that night with handsome Luigi in his dress uniform as the honored guest. She was grateful to Miss Bjorklund for this recognition. Antonetta was a loyal parent, she attended every Open School Night and loved to see her sons and daughters participating in plays, musical performances, and of course, progressing upward at graduation ceremonies.

I found Antonetta and Miss Bjorklund's relationship very interesting. I have always felt comfortable in school buildings and suspect it involved the positive interactions between the two of them. I took Mama's advice seriously and became a teacher.

As a newly arrived immigrant in May of 1929, she came to the land of plenty only to experience the Great Depression a few months later. Jobs were lost and there was little security in those that became available. But Antonetta was very much aware of the position teachers held at that time. She saw that teachers and postal employees kept their jobs. Teachers held respected positions in her experience.

Therefore, she strongly advised all of her children to become schoolteachers. She advised, "There were always open positions even in times of economic hardship." She wanted to see her children protected from the *miseria* she experienced in her early life. And so, although we had many talents and later in life explored different interests and occupations, we followed Mama's advice and became teachers.

As the baby, I followed in the footsteps of my siblings. I fondly remember how we ended each work week together. Every Friday we would all meet at Mama's house for a loaf of her freshly baked bread and a bottle of Papa's homemade wine to take home to our families. Our packages were lined up ready for us as we ate her delicious pizza just out of the oven and discussed our week at school and all the happenings in the New York City Board of Education. Mama beamed and was so proud that we listened to her practical advice. Yes, we, the Lombardis, became a family of public-school educators.

Antonetta and her friend, Comare Maria Tusiani, were both thrifty in handling household budgets. Not a single penny was wasted or overlooked. Theirs was a simple directive: savings was the order of the day. Everything that could be recycled was reused. In a large family such as ours, clothes were handed down to younger children. Mending was a common homemaker's task and the clothes we wore were often handmade. The dialect word *sparagna*, frugal, was the guiding economic philosophy. Both women had to survive life in a poor country as single women supporting their families when their husbands left Italy to find work in America.

For Mama it was six years with two young children, Grace and Angelo. For Comare Maria it was 24 years. During her years in Italy, she oversaw the education of her son, Joseph. He was a scholar who became a world-renowned writer and poet, publishing many books in Latin, Italian, English and his native Sammarchese dialect. He was also a musician and an international prize-winning poet.

Life changed for Antonetta and Maria when they came to America. And they quickly learned to navigate the bargain possibilities open to them in the Bronx. They knew how to adapt! Mama and Comare Maria somehow learned about Jewish merchants offering the best products at the lowest prices on Bathgate Avenue. This location required a train ride on the now defunct Third Avenue elevated line. They arranged to meet at the connecting subway station on Gun Hill Road. Although there was the expense of the train fare, the savings on their expenditures exceeded those they could find in local stores.

They came prepared to carry the many luscious fruits and vegetables in their sturdy shopping bags. These were no brown paper shopping bags that could be purchased for a nickel but their own sturdy homemade creations often refurbished from old window drapes, 10 pound flour sacks or any old household item they could redesign, Although I was embarrassed by these "different" shopping bags at the time, as I remember them now, they were actually elegant and often made from material having handsome floral patterns. Matha Stewart would be impressed.

The bargaining behavior of these two women was tried and true. They never paid the first price quoted by the Jewish merchants who spoke perfect Italian; and, of course, tasting was a must. Sometimes more grapes or cherries than was necessary were eaten to assess their quality causing negative rebukes from the shopkeepers. But this didn't phase Antonetta or Maria. Only the best was good enough for their families.

However, they were known to purchase brown bananas thought to be beyond their prime by some but whose sweetness was understood by others. Comare Maria's son, Michael, who became a highly successful international business leader tells what he calls the "brown banana story." As a child he was given a test at school and asked the color of a banana. Of course, he answered brown since that was his experience. His answer was quickly marked incorrect. Little did this educator understand of the immigrant experience.

I remember the short walk from the subway stop to the shoppers' paradise on Bathgate Avenue. The produce beautifully displayed at the store fronts had an enticing allure. It was all out there waiting for the discriminating shopper to make the deal. Dry goods stores were also represented on this avenue. What better place to buy socks and underwear at a reasonable price? These were examined carefully: what material were they made of, were the seams sewn properly, was the elastic strong? Time and patience were needed before a decision was made. And then bargaining began. I remember the unspoken communication between Mama and

Comare Maria when considering a purchase. The facial expressions summed it all up. They were their own mini quality consumer research team. Needless to say, they always agreed. They knew quality.

The trip home was fun because food samples were always given before the rosary beads came out for afternoon prayers on our train ride home. I know for Mama these were prayers of thanksgiving. We were taught to be thankful and appreciative for all we had. Antonetta was forever grateful for the "land of plenty" she was so fortunate to have come to those many years before.

In addition to her work as a dedicated homemaker and devoted mother, Antonetta had several "piecework" jobs outside the home. For many immigrant women of her time, extra money could be earned by sewing pieces: collars, sleeves, pockets, into sweaters, dresses or blouses for pennies an item. Angelo, the oldest child in the family, would tell us stories of how as a young boy he was her "delivery man" taking all the finished garments in his homemade wagon to the boss for payment. These employment possibilities were arranged on a very "informal" basis. However, her first legal job outside the home was in a television commercial in the early 1960s.

My sister Nan's friend, Mary Draper, worked for an advertising agency in New York City and got a big account with Rheingold Beer. This project was to run during the baseball world series games, and the theme was ethnic weddings. The ad concept was to target ethnic groups in New York to drink not only more beer but Rheingold Beer.

Mary was in charge of casting professional and non-professional actors for the Italian wedding ad. She called her Italian friends in a panic. By law, she needed real Italians to perform in the wedding scenes, the company needed experienced Italian wedding attendees. Professional actors were sometimes just too "slick." Nan and Thelma Palmieri, childhood friends of both my sisters Nan and Provie, agreed to recruit their family members.

Arrangements were made for taping at an upper east side restaurant for the day. Nan, having several gowns and was cast as a bridesmaid. Unfortunately, I was not yet 21 years old and so could not participate in an ad selling alcohol. Surprisingly, Mama was very interested in joining Nan. She had the perfect dress; her son Lou was recently married to Carol and her "mother of the groom" sea green dress was beautiful.

The simple bodice was elegantly decorated with crystal beads artfully sewn by her good Sammarchese friend, Molly Sassano.

Mama and Nan walked up to the avenue (White Plains Road and 219th Street) and took the IRT subway line into Manhattan. The restaurant was set with a live band playing Italian music, tables filled with delicious food and plenty of wine and beer recreating an authentic Italian wedding.

With a change of clothing and a makeup session they were ready. Antonetta was not thrilled with the makeup, but she was experienced at facing new challenges and she was there for work. She looked around and assessed the situation. She zoomed in on an old man and decided he would be her perfect dancing partner. Little did she know that he was one of the professional actors. When the band started playing the director told people to get into the "shot." Well, that was all that Mama had to hear. Although her English was limited, she clearly understood this prompt. Antonetta made sure that she was right in front of the camera dancing away with her new-found friend.

What did Papa think when he saw his traditional wife on television dancing with another man? Well, that's another story. Nan later shared that she was a bit taken aback because Mama was being so pushy and was constantly in front of the camera. She knew exactly how to enhance her role. After all, she was there for a job. And getting a job was of utmost importance in our family. Nan reported that Mrs. Palmieri, Thelma's mother, was not as aggressive and did not make the cut. The taping took eight hours which was no problem for Antonetta. She was accustomed to hard work and long hours on her little feet. The food, wine and music were free! And she was paid for the whole day's filming.

The director contacted Mary when they edited the tape and the next day she called Nan. "Your mother was the star of the commercial." The Italian Wedding was selected for the 1964 World Series and Antonetta became an "overnight" celebrity. Everyone recognized her in her tv debut. All the shopkeepers applauded as she entered their stores, and her family and friends were dazzled by her poise before the tv camera.

Upon reading a draft of this story, Margo, my niece, shared an experience her brother, Billy A had at Willy's bar. Billly A had just returned home after serving two tours in the Vietnam War and was enjoying an afternoon beer at Willy's. This old-time neighborhood bar was the local "watering hole" up on the avenue on 219th Street. Willy's was conveniently located at the bottom of the subway steps. It was a welcoming stop following a long day's work for all who traveled home on the IRT subway line, including his grandfather, Tough Tony.

Billy A sat on the bar stool in that dark cave-like space enjoying a cold beer and watching the Yankee game when suddenly, Mama popped up on the tv screen dancing away in the Rheingold Beer commercial. He shouted, "That's my grandma." At first the response from some of the other men sitting there was disbelief. The regulars knew him and his relationship to Papa, also a "patron" of this salty establishment. "Yes, that is Tony's wife." They all lifted their glasses, cheered and toasted Antonetta.

She earned royalties with each showing. Upon receiving her checks, she found it unbelievable that she didn't have to do another day's work and still earned money. Only in America!

Antonetta celebrated her success by cutting her long-braided hair and getting a perm, buying gold sandals and taking Papa by train, of course, on a sun-filled vacation to Florida. She also bought each of her children little gifts. Brother George, who was often called upon to represent us as the Lombardi family "attorney," shared that any actor in a role for a tv commercial who is on screen for a minimum of three seconds becomes a principal and is invited to be an honorary member of Actors Equity for one year with free membership. Now as a "professional actress" Mama was excited to join Actors Equity only because her favorite tv star, Perry Como, was a long-standing member.

At the time of her death when planning Antonetta's funeral in 1982, we met with Mr. Nick Romano, Director of Romano's Funeral Home, and were asked many questions about the "deceased." One was her profession. Nan and I looked at each other and knew there was only one answer to this question, we both exclaimed ACTRESS.

Years later our brother George researched the 1960's tv advertisements for Rheingold Beer. He found a family treasure. For Christmas he gave us all a copy of the commercial with Mama dancing before us in her major tv role. She traveled the road to stardom and was a smashing success!

Rheingold Beer Commercial
New York, NY 1964

Upon passing the Statue of Liberty in New York Harbor and reaching her new country, Antonetta immediately considered herself an American even before she stepped onto American soil. The long Atlantic crossing on the *Conte Grande* was over and she was ready to begin her new life in a new land. Brother Angelo loved to tell stories of his adventures on the maiden voyage of this beautiful new ship that left Naples on May 11, 1929.

After twenty-three busy years raising many children and running a large household Antonetta finally became a naturalized citizen. This was in 1954. And it was a few years later before she could vote. For Mama the 1960 election became a turning point.

The voting rights laws clearly set literacy standards for voting in the United States. All new voters had to demonstrate the ability to read and write in English. The New York State law allowed for two methods of qualification: "Read aloud intelligently from extracts containing the State Constitution and write ten words from such slips selected by the Inspector of Election **or** have notification from a school with a minimum of an eighth-grade education."

Antonetta was determined to vote for John F. Kennedy. She watched him on television and strongly felt that it was time for America to have a young person lead the country. He was so hopeful, so vital. And he had little children of his own. Mama was serious about her participation in this important election. For Antonetta there was only one way she could because she never attended school in the United States. She had to learn to read the important English words from the New York State Constitution. Antonetta had the confidence in learning these ten words even though her Italian writing skills limited her to phonetic spelling. However, she was convinced that she could make herself understood. We were sure that her enthusiasm and determination would be enough to make her qualify. Remember, she was born in 1901. Women in America did not get the right to vote until the 19th Amendment was ratified in 1920. Her experience of women's rights was not that of her daughters and grand-daughters.

Our brother, George, who was not formally trained as an attorney, was designated by all of us as the family "Advocate." He enthusiastically volunteered to help Mama pass the test. I remember the two of them sitting at the kitchen table practicing and all the hard work she devoted to achieving her goal. The date was set and we were all excited for her. She and George went to Public School 21 on East 225th street for Mama to take the test. She was very serious and driven. I can just imagine how she must have felt to finally be recognized as a true American citizen. She succeeded and was proud to now fully participate in the life of the country that had given her so much. Not only did she get the right to vote but the candidate she supported won the election! She was proud to know that her vote counted. The Lombardi household enthusiastically celebrated on that Election Day.

Only three years later as we all sat around the television watching the country's painful history unfold. Our president was killed. We were infused with the overwhelming grief of our beloved John Kennedy's tragic death. Mama mournfully sat there reciting her rosary and together we witnessed our Papa's tears. This was their country and their president.

Antonetta sewed most of the clothes for her children on her faithful Singer sewing machine. For her there were two modes of dress: house clothing and outside clothing. There is an Italian expression, *bella figura,* which means looking good or making a good appearance in public. Italians love to observe people from head to toe. What you wear is important for the impression you make. On a visit to Italy our ten-year old daughter, Meg, was bothered by the "looking." She said, "everyone is staring at me." I explained that this was cultural behavior. Everyone stares at everyone. Italians love people. They have a natural curiosity about others. There is something interesting about each of us. Besides, what would they have to gossip about?

Our Italian cousins were constantly changing their clothes. Simple clothes for the house and lovely silk dresses and leather shoes for outside, even to the open food market. I couldn't imagine what they thought of us wearing jeans, sweatshirts and sneakers all day even when we are out in public! Were they perhaps thinking that Americans have no sense of personal pride?

Mama adored all her children. She considered each of them absolutely beautiful and wanted them to make a good appearance. Although there was not much money to buy clothes, we always wore something presentable when we went outside. The clothing was always clean, starched and pressed. Our inside clothes were usually worn and ill-fitting but serviceable for all the jobs we were assigned in running a large household.

Mama relaxed the outside clothes rule for Carey and Andrew, my sister Provie's two children. When my brother-in-law, Bob, would bring them to visit Antonetta she had "hand me downs" ready for them to wear. She was always considerate and did not want to send them home with soiled clothes. Play clothes were for having fun even if that meant getting them dirty. Thinking back, I suspect the neighbors must have thought that they came from a poor family judging from the shabby clothes they wore playing in grandma's yard.

On special occasions such as the first day of the school year or on special holidays, extra attention was given to the outfits we wore. This was the case for me in 1953 when I made my First Holy Communion. The sacraments of the Catholic Church were deeply meaningful to Antonetta, and I was approaching an important one. My mother made me a beautiful dress for this milestone. Mama, my older sister Provie, (who designed and sewed many of her own elegant clothes) and I walked up the avenue to the dry goods shop to purchase just the right fabric. In addition to the two fabrics used, Provie insisted that we splurge and buy a Vogue pattern for this dress. The dress had a classic round collar, with short puffy sleeves, a scalloped overskirt, a delicately embroidered organdy underskirt and a thick tie that became a pretty bow to grace the back of the dress. When we got home, measurements were taken, and Mama couldn't wait to cut out the pattern. She and Provie continually evaluated the design and when they were both satisfied Mama was ready to begin sewing.

This was so exciting to me as a young girl. I was thrilled by the extra effort made in its creation. I remember feeling so special – my dress was made with care and love, and I truly felt like the little angel my mother envisioned. All of this attention was unusual for me because as the youngest child of a large family I rarely wore something new and certainly nothing that required this amount of work and expense. *Bella figura* was definitely the order of the day in wearing this dress.

Years later, when we traveled to New York City to purchase my wedding dress, I selected the very first one I tried on at Lord & Taylor, a popular department store. Its fabric and delicate Swiss lace brought back the magic of my communion dress. I knew I had found the perfect one.

The story of the dress did not end with my Communion. In 1971 after the birth of our son, Paul, Antonetta had another use in mind. My husband, Charles was serving as the minister of his first church in North Attleboro, Massachusetts at the time. Mama came up from the Bronx to spend a week helping her baby – me – with the care of her first-born child. She surprised me by bringing my Communion dress. She had saved it in a beautiful box that was lined with white tissue paper. She was convinced that this dress would have another life. Antonetta offered to redesign it as Paul's baptismal gown. I was touched and she was ready for the task.

After I was married Mama bought me a portable sewing machine. She believed every married woman had to possess this essential tool. She used my machine to sew the baptismal gown. She also made two under slips; a blue one for her grandson, Paul and a white one if I had a girl "one day." Yes, she was always forward looking. Antonetta artfully cut the fabric and created a unique gown using the organdy embroidered skirt from my communion dress. This was such a powerful link to my past. After Paul's celebration the gown was packed away and saved for the next grandchild. Our daughter, Meg was born three years later, and she carried on the tradition of wearing grandma's dress on her christening day. We still have the dress, and it was worn by Antonetta's great granddaughters, Isabel and Maisy. Little did Mama and Provie know that they had created an heirloom and that it would be lovingly passed onto future generations. I am sure they both are smiling down from heaven knowing their spirit is present today and that their love will forever sustain me.

After Mama's death her children met to share her few possessions. We agreed that I should take Mama's Singer sewing machine. This machine had a special place in our home. It lived in an alcove next to the kitchen. We saw it every day. I have cherished memories of Antonetta sewing and mending for all of us.

To my surprise, in reading her will we found *"la machine singer per cucire è di Teresa"* (the Singer sewing machine is Teresa's). These were her words, written clearly in her strong hand and reaching out to me in 2025 forty-three years after her death, when we discovered her will among my brother Lou's saved documents.

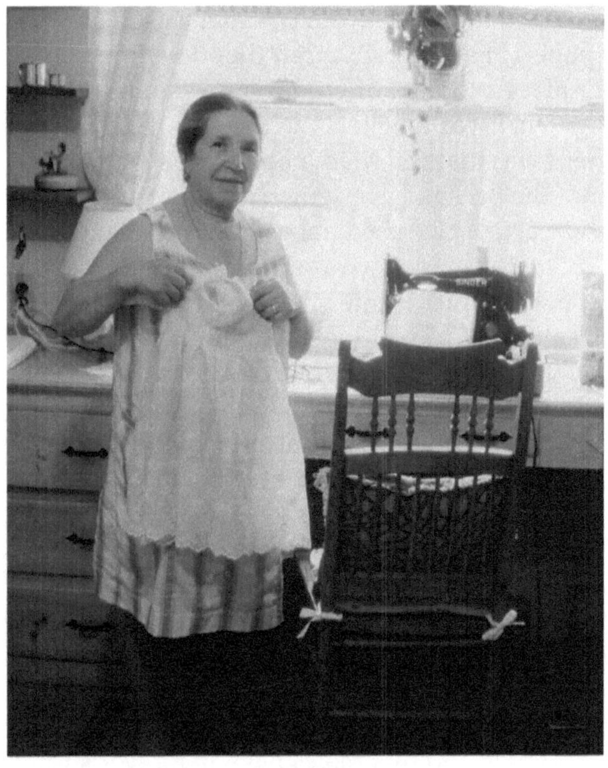

Antonetta Sews the Christening Dress
North Attleboro, MA 1971

Elaine Evans was a dear friend from our years in Brooklyn when my husband, Charles, served as minister of the All Souls Universalist Church, a Unitarian Universalist Church located on Ocean Avenue. Our son Paul and her son Gideon attended the same nursery school and became best buddies. Elaine loved to tell the story of how we met. The director of the school introduced us, and we soon discovered that not only were we neighbors in Brooklyn, but we also were next door neighbors in Springs, a hamlet in the town of East Hampton, New York, where we spent our summers and coincidentally both had husbands named Charles! This was just the beginning of our many connections.

Each year Elaine and Charles graciously hosted their famous Evans brunch at their East Hampton home. Elaine's father, Morris Pitt and her mother Sara would bring bagels, smoked salmon, white fish salad, herring and other delectable treats catering a fabulous feast of delicious food we all savored from Brooklyn.

Mama visited us each summer and gladly accepted the invitation to brunch. She and Elaine's mother, Sara, immediately bonded. Although they were from different cultures, they had so much in common. Both left the old country, Mama from Italy and Mrs. Pitt from Poland. Both were born in the beginning of the twentieth century. They experienced early years of poverty and the difficult and often devastating circumstances that poor European immigrants faced. They became enthusiastic American citizens in the land of opportunity with so many resources available to them, their children and grandchildren. Just think, Mrs. Pitt's son Harvey became Chairman of the Securities and Exchange Commission and was sworn in at the Supreme Court Building in Washington, DC. An unbelievable honor for a poor immigrant from Poland.

Mama's English was limited, and Mrs. Pitt spoke with a heavy accent, but they managed to communicate for hours on end. Mama and Mrs. Pitt came dressed in their East Hampton chic, outfits of ruffled blouses, long flowing skirts, sensible shoes and for Mama comfortable white ankle socks. Our mothers enjoyed sharing their history, their joys and their sorrows. They understood each other's pain and pride in their children and grandchildren. Although they came from different backgrounds and religious traditions, they connected easily. Elaine was amazed that her mother told Antonetta her age, a secret she did not even share with her own family.

Together, the two friends approached the table laden with special treats. Mama had her own style of bagel eating. As one friend observed, she made a bagel hero, one filled with lox, cream cheese, onions, tomato, whitefish salad, and of course, a piece of lettuce for the necessary daily greens. Mr. Pitt was delighted and so proud of what he saw – the enjoyment his food brought to all the adults and many children attending. What were the thoughts of this Polish immigrant, living with early years of hunger and now witnessing the plentiful bounty he was able to provide to so many on those sunny summer mornings?

Elaine, my sister Nan, who also had a summer house in the Springs, and I would often reminisce while sitting on Atlantic Beach about the instant friendship between Mama and Mrs. Pitt. They were both women who transitioned from the old world to the new, from poverty to the good life, from fractured homes at an early age to the joy of being surrounded by loving families in their mature years. Yes, they had much in common. And I have years of precious memories, memories of our dear friends Elaine and Charles, raising our children together and sharing milestones as they grew into adulthood. The Evans family is such an important part of our summer years on Underwood Drive, one I will always cherish.

Antonetta Goes to Argentina Armed and Ready

WWII caused tremendous upheaval for Italians. After the war, economic conditions forced many to leave their homeland and migrate to other countries. Zia Caterina, Papa's youngest sister, and her husband chose Argentina. This South American country attracted many Europeans. Jobs were plentiful and the culture was familiar.

Zia Caterina created a new life there and four of her children were born in Argentina. Antonetta maintained regular correspondence using the lightweight blue airmail paper to share news with her sister-in-law. Mama also sent packages with clothing and medicines as she had to our relatives in Italy. Although Mama and Papa were not affluent by any means, Papa worked more regularly after the Depression, and they understood the needs of their struggling relatives. Thousands of miles separating them but the ties to family were never broken.

In 1978, a few years after her husband's death, Antonetta was ready for another trip. All on her own she planned her new adventure. She knew of an Italian travel agent on White Plains Road and decided that this was a good place to begin. She went prepared with Zia Caterina's address in Argentina and explained her wishes to visit a sister-in-law she knew well but hadn't seen in more than forty-seven years. I am sure this was a wish he often heard from his immigrant clientele.

Antonetta came home and announced to her family that she was going to Argentina ALONE! The family was shocked that a woman of her age with significant language barriers should plan such a trip so far away from her home. We understood her affection for Zia Caterina but were surprised that our Mama had made all the arrangements herself without consulting any of us and had her tickets in hand for this long trip to another continent. Serious planning commenced in earnest. She contacted Zia Caterina and her family and then the packing commenced. The two women were thrilled at the prospect of being reunited. They had both been transplanted to new worlds and had so much to share. Their lives were so different from those they had in the small village nestled in the mountains of San Marco in Lamis. They both now lived in new lands and very different cultures.

The departure date was set, and Antonetta's children were all so nervous: was she going to be safe, how would she navigate this long plane ride, how would she get from the airport to our aunt's house, how would she communicate in a different language? Antonetta was not worried at all. Everything would work out for her. She was not afraid. She was ready for what would be one of the major events of her mature life. She was courageous in knowing she could do this herself.

We all wanted to see Mama off on her trip to South America. A convoy of cars filled with children and grandchildren arrived at the airport. Her bags were checked, and last-minute advice was carefully given to a very calm traveler. She proceeded to the gate and all of a sudden, a screeching alarm sounded as Antonetta passed through the security. Her pocketbook had to be searched. What was she carrying that caused the security alarm to go off? Well, she had decided it would be a good idea to take a scissor with her. Now this was not just any ordinary cutting tool but the largest tailoring scissor she owned. It was at least ten or twelve inches in length! Her children were aghast and definitely embarrassed.

Why did she feel she needed this monstrous scissor? Her answer was simply: "Well, you never know." She was armed. She always wanted to be prepared. Of course, it was taken away at the gate. She continued walking to the plane unfazed by the whole incident. We discreetly spoke to the stewardess requesting her to "look out" for Mama on her flight. No problem, everything would be fine. We left the airport laughing and crying at the same time.

Everything was fine. Antonetta arrived safely and she began the visit she was dreaming about, one of reconnecting with her past, rejoining Papa's little sister and meeting her new nieces and nephew for the first time. Mama and Zia Caterina spent a month talking, talking, talking. They shared a bed and talked through the night. There was so much they had to tell each other. They last saw each other as young women and were now old. They were reconnecting after the birth of children and grandchildren and death of both their husbands. Antonetta was thrilled by her experiences in Argentina, especially in helping to cook meals for the large extended family. Since Tonino, one of our cousins, was a rancher, barbeque was a culinary tradition. Mama loved it and joyfully told us how she and Zia Caterina chopped endless amounts of garlic and mint to flavor the delicious beef. Her Argentine family embraced Antonetta and maintained a strong emotional connection with her until her death. Again, we were reminded of Mama's courage and wisdom in bravely making decisions and following through on dreams. We continue to correspond with our cousins and our brother, George, and his wife Toni, were fortunate to have traveled to South America to visit with them.

When Antonetta returned home, she had no voice. We immediately took her to the doctor. Did she catch some exotic germ on her trip? My sister, Nan, even took her to a specialist in New York City. We were worried. The diagnosis was a simple one: overworked vocal cords! She had so much to catch up on and knew her time there was limited. She simply spent a month talking, talking, talking.

An amusing memory of that trip was a discussion I had with Mama when she returned home about her experience on the airplane. Previously, her first and only plane ride had been on a short trip to Boston when she and Nan came to visit me in North Attleboro, Massachusetts. Antonetta was enthusiastic about flying. Soaring high up in the sky was a marvel for her. Remember she was born in 1901 and was witness to many new technological advancements.

We talked about the long plane ride to Argentina and sleeping during the trip. She said that there were no issues with men and women being together. I asked why there would be any problem. She answered saying that she couldn't fall asleep in her dress because it would get wrinkled. I was bracing myself for the explanation of this comment. She told me that she took off her dress and carefully folded it in her lap. "After all, her dress was black and her slip was black so there was no problem, you couldn't see anything." I just shook my head in disbelief and was so happy I was not there to witness Mama's practical solution in maintaining an unwrinkled dress on a transcontinental flight.

Upon some reflection, I realized the whole wrinkled dress thing was really driven by Mama's Italian culture. *La bella figure*, making a good impression, explains why she wanted to look her best upon first seeing Zia Caterina and her children. Antonetta was a modest person and a very practical one. But she was also concerned with her image. Meeting her Argentine family in a wrinkled dress was simply unthinkable!

I was the last of nine children born to my mother at age 44 and my father at age 50, Antonetta often called me her "change-of-life baby." In 1945 forty-four was considered elderly for a woman to give birth to a child. I always enjoyed being introduced by my brothers and sisters as the baby of our family. However, at this point in my life I occupy the family position with sadness. I have had to witness the death of five siblings. Now there are only two of us left, George and "baby" Theresa. We hold Antonetta's history close to our hearts. What will happen to her legacy when we are no longer here to tell her stories? Will the lessons she taught be lost? Dear reader, what will happen to your stories, your family history, when you're gone?

Although I am the baby of a large family, I am the one whom fate has chosen to report on the past. As the cherished last child I had a very different relationship with my parents than my siblings did. Their lessons in child rearing and the traditional Italian practices of the past sometimes proved painful. I have seen the changes in their behaviors and have a view of the lives of my immigrant parents over a long period of time. From their first child, Angelo, to me, the baby of the family, child rearing practices changed dramatically in our immigrant home. My siblings love to tell me how they didn't even know that Mama was pregnant with me until the day she came home from the hospital with this "beautiful baby sister."

Angelo, who was 24 years my senior, was in the Navy and didn't know his mother was pregnant again. At sea he was ordered to report to the captain of the ship. He then got a special message from his wife, Millie, informing him of my birth. Can you just imagine the shock? Well, "life goes on."

As the first-born daughter, my sister, Grace, was held more strictly to the old codes. After all, she was born in Italy.

When she fell in love with her handsome soldier, Bill Cornelius, who was on leave in New York, there was an immediate upheaval in the family. First, he was not Italian and second, he was a stranger. He came from Kentucky and was in the army stationed in Oklahoma City. Who were his people, what were his values, what kind of a husband would he be? He wasn't even Catholic! Grace was a maverick. She would not be held back from her dream, from her love and finally had the courage to act. She bravely found her voice. Grace made the painful decision. Grace and Bill eloped! Wow, this was a bombshell and required many hours of prayer by Antonetta. Grace purposely timed her elopement immediately after the wedding of her older brother. He was was home on special leave for his marriage to Millie. Grace knew everyone would be busy planning the celebration in the short time granted and Angelo would be home for only a few days for a special matrimonial leave. This all happened in 1944 while World War II was still in process. Angelo was serving in the Navy, assigned to a tanker, the USS Salamonie in the Pacific theater.

The wedding provided a substantial distraction for Grace's audacious act as she and Bill got on a train and traveled many, many miles away. Mama was heartbroken and Papa was furious. His children did not defy him! This just did not happen in San Marco. Well, Papa followed them, he made that trip out West to Bill's army base and I can only imagine what happened next. Whatever it was, he came back satisfied that she made a good choice and Bill was forever welcomed into the family.

In fact, Mama and Bill had a special relationship and were very much in harmony. Perhaps the fact that they were both orphaned at a young age, lived on a farm and survived the economic hardships that molded their lives. Deprivation prepared them to cope with the struggles they were sure to face. Grace's first child was born in September of

1945, two months after my birth. I wonder how my mother felt being pregnant at the same time as her eldest daughter? And how did her daughter feel? I can't believe we never discussed this.

Grace's marriage made Provie's marriage to Antonetta's first Jewish son-in-law easy; as well as my marriage at the young age of eighteen. Our spouses were judged only as individuals who could be devoted husbands. Provie's rebellion and insistence as a woman to attend college, an unusual act in our immigrant community, later made it a requirement for the younger daughters of the family, The fear of what other people might think changed with time.

Antonetta's childrearing years were very busy indeed. She worked hard. She prayed hard with rosary beads always in her apron pocket. As her children got older and left the house, she had more time for me. I listened to her stories. Some were sweet but some were downright scary. *Hansel and Gretal* Italian style borders on horror. I can still feel the fear I felt back then when I think of Mama's version. As a young child I went everywhere with Mama no matter what the task or place. There were no babysitters in my young life. I felt so lucky to have her all to myself. She taught me to be independent, to be practicable, to be brave, to shop, to cook, to bake, to sew, to dance, to pray, to love and to remember.

Mama's old passport photograph was taken in 1929. The picture is black-and-white and has been copied many times for her children, grandchildren, and great-grandchildren. Her formal pose communicates seriousness. She is looking directly at the photographer with a yearning. I know there was a photographer in San Marco because my oldest brother Angelo told me a story, and yes, repeated it many times, of the picture he had taken as a young boy to be sent to Papa in America. He was placed on a tricycle in the photo studio. Having little money, a substantial toy such as this was one he surely never had. After the photo session Angelo was told to get off the tricycle. He refused and created quite a scene. He thought the tricycle was now his and went into a tantrum causing such excitement that this same photographer who took Mama's passport picture a few years later was sure to remember her wild boy.

In the picture Mama is probably wearing the one nice dress she owned. She is wearing a pearl necklace and pearl drop earrings. I look at her jewelry in bewilderment. I never saw these pearls in her jewelry box. Did my father send her these pearls from America or were they another of the photographer's props to enhance the portrait? I wish this photograph could talk. Looking and wondering, it's always the eyes that I am drawn to. Those endearing eyes reach out to me like a magnet, *figlia bella,* dear daughter.

In the photo Mama's hair is neatly combed in a braided bun, very "old world." This was the traditional hairstyle of the women in her village. Her braided bun was held together with long bone hairpins. These I now keep as one of Mama's precious gifts to me, beloved mementos that are now packed away for safekeeping in a black velvet pouch. Occasionally I take them out and remember how she wore them. I remember as a child watching Mama comb her long wavy hair in the sunlight as it dried after shampooing. Her hair was long and beautiful; it flowed to her waist. She braided it using her nimble little fingers in time to the old folk song she was singing to me. These braids were twirled at the base of her head and secured with the hairpins.

Mama's hairstyle was not at all like that of my friends' moms. Their moms had the silky pageboy styles of the gorgeous women in the Breck Shampoo magazine advertisements of the 1950s. Mama was different. My mother was 44 years old when I was born. I was the last of her nine children and a surprise. She often referred to me as her "change-of-life baby." She was the oldest mother of the students in my elementary school classes at the P.S. 13. Some of my classmates would ask, "is that your grandmother?" Her old-world style made her look even older. Actually, she really was a grandmother at that time. My nephew Billy A, my sister Grace's son, who is two months younger than me, was also in my classes throughout elementary school.

I can remember feeling embarrassed but not for long. There were so many things that were different about my immigrant parents compared to those of my American friends. My mother always wore an apron, baked her own breads, canned her own tomatoes, sewed our clothes and always had rosary beads close at hand. My father made wine in the cellar, hunted for wild mushrooms, and caught long black eels which he brought home alive. They were released from their burlap bags to swim in our bathtub. And we had a big bountiful fig tree in our back yard. Each year he wrapped the huge fig tree in old blankets and coats and crowning it with a dented pail completing the look of an absurd sculpture protecting the homestead during the cold months ahead. In Italy the fig trees did not require this winter wrapping. None of my American friends had seen this before.

The 27-year-old woman in the old photograph faced many changes in her 81 years of life. She left her life of *miseria*, poverty. In Italy she lived in a one room stone house with a fireplace for warmth and cooking. There was no running water, electricity or central heating. As an orphan she had to leave the village and live on a farm. Her marriage gave her the gift of family. She felt blessed with each new child, grandchild and great grandchild. What is remarkable is how easily Mama transitioned to her new life. She was never afraid of new things, meeting new people, traveling to new places, experiencing new ways of doing things. She proudly became an American citizen and diligently voted in every election thereafter.

Antonetta's photographs also evolved into a new life. We now have VCR images of Mama as an actress in Rheingold Beer television advertisements. Fortunately, we now have family albums containing many endearing pictures of Mama documenting a woman's life well lived.

Antonetta's old photograph is more than a mere image on a printed page. We have a face to connect to the name. Loving memories stay with us and can be shared with those who never knew this extraordinary person. Mama will always be staring back bravely. She was a real person. We will always have a connection to her, and her story will continue generation after generation. If we remember and become entangled in her stories, our Antonetta will not be forgotten.[1]

---

[1] The "old photograph" on this book's front cover was taken for Antonietta's Italian passport in 1929.

PART THREE

Lessons on Death

Antonetta spoke to us about death even as young children. For her death was a natural part of life. It was not to be feared but to be courageously faced. As a family, we were taught to "pay our respects" at wakes and funerals, no matter what our age. Sometimes we were expected to kiss the corpse goodbye! I remember clearly the stone-cold skin of these encounters. This behavior was not considered at all unusual in our immigrant community.

Mama's first two children born in America died as infants. They were very close in age. Michelina died in 1931 from an infection that resulted from her ear piercing. Lucia died in 1932 also because of an infection. Hers was caused by a burn to her leg – a little leg that accidentally touched the hot potbelly stove used for heating. Remember, this was a period before penicillin or any other antibiotics needed to treat infections. It is hard to believe because today we deal with even more serious infections so easily.

I have greatly benefited from modern medicine. The drugs I take have made me well and keep me healthy. The experimental cancer treatment I received at the Smilow Cancer Hospital at Yale in a clinical trial under the brilliant care of Dr. Joseph Kim has exceeded my expectations and prayers. I am awestruck by the dramatic difference in the state of medicine today and that which was available to the immigrants of my mother's time. I don't know how Mama handled the deaths of her babies because it was well before I was born. I only know her affection for these little daughters was forever a part of her life and they were always remembered in her prayers.

Michelina and Lucia are buried in St. Raymond's Cemetery in the Bronx. Also included in this plot is Michele Cipriani, one of my father's distant relatives who died when he was only fifty-two years old. My father took responsibility for Michele's funeral arrangements because he was a bachelor, and Papa was his only relative in America. I was four years old at the time of his death and not yet in school. While Papa was at work Mama had to be present for all the funeral arrangements. Our family went to old man Romano, the funeral director, for his help. He drove me and Mama to the morgue to identify Michele. I clearly remember his body being slid out on a silver slab. A white cloth was removed from his face for Antonetta to identify him. As a child I found it interesting that he still had his mustache. And then I remember him being brought back to the funeral home to prepare him for the wake. He was lying on a platform draped in a red velvet mantle until a casket was selected. Mama prayed and I played.

Wow, you must be asking, dear reader, what kind of a mother Antonetta was, how could she expose her young daughter to the whole morgue experience, allowing her to sit there with a small box of crayons quietly coloring so close to a dead body? Mama's view of death was not scary or morbid. We were taught not to be frightened. Death is a reality in our lives. Antonetta knew this and certainly did Mr. Romano who dealt with it almost every day. I was simply included in an important life experience. I never had any nightmares or bad dreams about this, but I distinctly recall the details almost seventy-six years later. The red velvet is still a deep, rich color, and its texture was regal; it was beautiful. And Mr. Romano's kindness is something I also remember all these years later.

Tragically, in 1958, Antonetta had to face the death of a third daughter, Providenza. Provie was Mama's third child born in America in 1933. She died because of a medical accident at the age of twenty-five, leaving a distraught and loving husband, Bob Weiss, and two young children: a daughter, Carey, 15 months old, and a son, Andrew, three months old. Her death was caused by the careless mis-labeling of blood by a hospital technician. Panic surrounded this death.

I was twelve-years old and remember that dark night when the family came home from the hospital. What happened? Why was everyone so angry? When I was told I could not believe it, I could not comprehend that my beloved sister, Provie, had died that night. She was described by my oldest sister, Grace, as "looking radiant lying on that stark white sheet, with tears on her cheeks, and her hair in a long thick braid. She looked so tiny in her hospital bed."

Papa could not control his fury. He came home looking for his shotgun. He wanted to shoot the doctor, kill the person responsible for his daughter's death. I remember seeing my oldest brother, Angelo, holding Papa back and being forceful and direct with him. This was totally out of character for Angelo. He was the firstborn, always obedient and submissive to his strong-willed Papa. Now he was controlling his father and trying to manage his rage and pain.

Antonetta came home with the family and did not say a word. She immediately went down to the basement, her realm, her domain. The cellar kitchen belonged to her, and it was where she was in control – where she baked bread and cooked our meals. She labored to wash all the family's laundry using her old-fashioned wringer washing machine.

I later understood that this was the only way she could deal with her anguish, with her agony. Mama had to spend the entire night working hard in the basement by herself, washing clothes and saying prayers aloud. She had to be especially strong since Papa had completely fallen apart. Something we had never experienced before. But Antonetta did not have the luxury of tears and deep mourning that night. She had to do something practical that brought fortitude to the painful burden she was carrying. Somehow, she had to face the painful loss of her precious Providenza, the family star who was always at the top of her class at school. The trailblazer who insisted on going to college, setting this standard for women in the family at a time when this was not an accepted path for the daughters of other Italian immigrants.

Mama knew she had to be strong for all of us. We were now a shattered family. We were certainly not prepared for such an unexpected and wrenching loss. Throughout Provie's wake and funeral, Mama was dignified. She maintained her inner control. She had to make the unbearable bearable. She was responsible for many other lives. Her God had to guide her once again.

We were all so broken that we could never speak about Provie. The pain of separation was always with us. Our silence about her almost made Provie a ghost in our midst. This was a mistake. Provie's husband, Bob, was a giant of a man. His mother, Elizabeth, although non-Italian speaking, became Antonetta's closest ally in this war on misery. They communicated in few words but were able to emotionally brace each other as they faced the distress and suffering ahead. Bob understood us. He unconditionally maintained and nourished our continued relationship with him and his two very young children. Although we were culturally so different, we were bonded by Provie's love.

Years later, when he married Olga, we as a family were so happy to have her in our lives, and for Carey and Andrew now to have a mother again. She embraced our crazy Italian family just as fully as we embraced her.

Antonetta did not have the same difficulty talking about Providenza. In fact, she visited her grave almost every Sunday at Woodlawn Cemetery, trimming the ivy she had planted there, saying her prayers and talking to her dear lost daughter. Death had found her again and she faced it with unbelievable courage and resolve. Her response to disappointment and sadness was to shrug her shoulders saying "what are you going to do?" She often repeated this lament when life brought us unreasonable, if not unbearable realities.

Lombardi Family Celebrates Provie & Bob's Marriage
Top: Bob, Provie, Bill, Grace, Nan, Angelo, Mama,
Millie, Papa, Carol, George, Lou
Bottom: Lucille, Theresa, BillyA, Margo.
Last picture of the Lombardi family together in
New York City 1954

Something terrible happened. I remember it was in the middle of the night and members of my family came into the house suffocating in a cloak of sadness, anger and fear. The date was February 22, 1958, Mama's 57th birthday. My sister Provie only 25 years old with two small babies, died at St. John's Hospital in Yonkers. I was shaken by fear. A place for healing became a place of death. Mama's birthday was never celebrated again. I learned that things could go wrong in the right places.

Fear of hospitals and of medical care became part of the family's psychic make up. Medical accidents are a reality even today. We knew we had to be on guard and never allow a family member to face medical treatment alone, not at a doctor's office, not a treatment facility, not in a hospital. Our family promise was to always have a protective chaperone with us, to be their "eagle eyes."

Get ready for another experience of fear in a medical setting. Fortunately for me, our daughter Meg wanted me there for the birth of her two children. I was allowed to be in the birthing room with her husband, Chris. The ultimate joy is to witness the birth of a grandchild. In 2011 Meg's second child, a daughter, Nina, was born on my birthday, on a warm July day. My birthday brought back the memory of Provie's death on Mama's birthday. Childbirth could be dangerous even in 2011.

I was on an emotional roller coaster of excitement and fear. I called in all my most powerful prayers. I mentally projected a golden aura surrounding Meg in her hospital bed as she progressed through labor with control and grace. Pain management was discussed, and the choice was made for her good friend Frank Johnson, a senior anesthesiologist at Holy Cross Hospital in Silver Spring, Maryland, to help. His decision was to administer an epidural. I could not watch Frank place that long needle in Meg's spine. Could anything go wrong? Could she remain paralyzed? I had to "keep quiet" and just stand to the side. I didn't want to be told to leave. Thankfully, this went well, and Nina was delivered.

However, as she was easing out to meet us there was a serious problem, her umbilical cord was wrapped twice around her neck. She was in danger! Her doctor, a former Navy surgeon, acted quickly and cut the cord. I was standing just beside him, and we made quick eye contact. I felt paralyzed but had to maintain control which I didn't think was possible. Nina was rushed to the NICU (newborn intensive care unit) because she needed to be stabilized and had to receive the special nutrients that are transmitted through the umbilical cord during delivery. We all remained calm and were assured that signs indicated our eight-pound beauty was a healthy baby girl and would easily respond to the treatment.

Hold on! We are not at the scary part yet. I stayed with Meg in the hospital, sleeping in a chair by her side. Her husband, Chris, went home to be with their five-year-old son, Nico. Meg was still under the effect of the epidural and could not walk. She needed a wheelchair to go from her room to the NICU during the night to breastfeed Nina. Well, if you want to see miracles of modern medicine just visit the NICU. Tiny babies, some weighing only one pound, were in the delicate care of a gifted medical staff using incredible technologies to keep these dear little ones alive and growing. Here we were with our "fat" Nina surrounded by her peers who were struggling to survive. She did not need the oxygen in one of those special cribs or all the tubes desperately connecting her to life. She only needed the extra medicine to energize her immune system. We felt so thankful.

I was tense all day. Meg asked, "Why are you so nervous, you just got the best birthday gift of all, a beautiful granddaughter?" I then visited my past and told her about my sister Provie's death on Mama's birthday. We looked at the clock, it was 11:30 p.m. Suddenly a nurse came in wearing an unusual vest. It was bright yellow and had six oversized pockets. Each pocket was intended to hold a baby in case of an emergency. She calmly told us there was a fire in the hospital and we had to evacuate. As Meg and I looked into each other's eyes we knew what we had to do but we were frightened. We faced that fear together. Meg could not walk. She had to remain in the wheelchair. The nurse gently placed Nina on her lap and I was to guide her out of the hospital. There were too many babies for the nurses' vests. Although it was risky, I volunteered to help. I told Meg "You hold Nina and another baby, and I will take one and push the wheelchair."

We were planning our exit when we received word that the courageous firefighters, stationed only one block away, had quickly controlled the fire in the nearby elevator shaft. We did not have to evacuate after all. We were given a pass. The time was 11:59, still my birthday. My daughter and granddaughter were safe!

What would have happened if the fire was not controlled? What would have happened to Meg and Nina if I weren't there to help? Later in the early morning hours when we went back to Meg's hospital room we had to pass the elevator shaft. There was a huge hole in the floor and charred walls. The elevator was destroyed. We could smell the smoke and there was a narrow walkway for us to get by. How would we have managed our escape from this fire? I had to leave these thoughts aside and concentrate on getting Meg to her room and in a bed.

Blood clots or serious bleeding sometimes result after childbirth and as directed by the busy nurses I had to be sure Meg was placed in a reclining position in bed. After hours of childbirth and the fearful experience of the hospital fire we needed quiet time. Meg, Nina and I were safe. I was relieved that I was there. I was grateful that I was able to conquer my fear. On that day thoughts of Mama were constant. My July birthday passed without tragedy.

Antonetta did not receive a birthday gift on that cold February 22nd night. She was given profound pain that forever seared a "hole in her heart." Her heart was forced to stoically carry yet another hurt; another loss, another death, this one on her birthday, one she had to endure and had to painfully pray to accept.

EIGHTY-ONE IS ENOUGH

How does one decide when life is complete, and it is time to die? Reaching her eighty-first year Mama calmly told us it was her last. "Eighty-one is enough," she said. She was a devout Catholic with a sustaining belief in life after death. She was not afraid of dying. She was ready. I almost felt she willed her death. How did she make this decision with such grounding and determination? First, she explained that "Papa lived to this age, if it was enough time for him, it was enough for me."

Perhaps being born in 1901 gives one this attitude toward old age and death. After all, many people she loved died young. Second, she was beginning to forget. Her memory was slowly being compromised. For Antonetta, this was totally unacceptable. She was an independent person and loved her freedom. Mama lived in her own apartment and was in control of her finances, personal decisions, and her life. She now had to face a new stage. Loss of memory brought loss of control.

She often told us how grateful she was to President Franklin D. Roosevelt. He made it possible for her to receive Social Security benefits, providing her with financial security and medical coverage. Antonetta did not have to depend on anyone, especially her children, for her survival. She was in charge. This was such an advancement for someone who was orphaned as a child of the early twentieth century with no resources except the kindness of others. As a result of the early death of her parents, it must have seemed that everything had come to an end. No family, no home, no education. In Italy of 1909, you could only continue attending school beyond the third grade if you could pay for tuition and books. The vast majority could not. Antonetta's education abruptly ended when she was only eight years old. She knew firsthand the importance of formal education and instilled its value in all her children, especially the females. Her constant message to her daughters was that they must have a career, earn their own money and be financially independent. We understood her feelings on her eighty-first birthday. She loved to travel, and death would be the ultimate spiritual journey. Mama was ready.

As she grew older, she faced many changes, and her life was very different in 1981. Emigration to America provided the opportunity for an improved life. After a long marriage to the handsome, hard-working man she loved she was left with resources of her own. With the help of her son, George, she sold her house in the Bronx and went to live in a comfortable first-floor apartment in Yonkers. An added benefit was that her loving son, Lou, owned this five-family dwelling which provided her a secure and friendly environment. Although she did not drive, here she could walk to every important location on her list: church, stores, doctor, dentist. Or, she could easily take a bus. She even had a clothesline outside her kitchen window! Just down the street on McLean Avenue, Mama had a comfortable bench facing the afternoon sun. This was also a resting spot after long walks. It also gave her the added benefit for people-watching, a favorite Italian pastime.

Mama taught us to "joy" (enjoy) our lives. She was easy to please and easy to entertain. Antonetta took pleasure in life experiences. At weddings she gladly danced the *Tarantella*, playing her ancient wooden castanets. She brought them with her from Italy. She told me they were made by her father. Made from wood found in the mountains surrounding San Marco. They are one of the few possessions saved after her mother's death. Mama gave them to me because I was named after my grandmother and passed them on honoring an old tradition. They are one of my most valued possessions. I sometimes hold them, close my eyes, and try to feel the past, longing for the connection to a life and people beyond my own. Antonetta loved music and enjoyed watching her favorite television shows featuring Perry Como and Lawrence Welk.

Mama was an independent woman who took charge of her own life. And it was not surprising that Wonder Woman, "Linda" as she referred to her, was her favored superhero. Antonetta faced death with the same strength and dignity she demonstrated throughout her life. Papa died six years earlier, and now she was ready to follow. She told us it was time for her to die. Time for her to move on. Time for her to join all those she loved and lost. As a pious and devout Catholic, she believed in a spiritual life after death – in a rebirth, a new beginning, a homecoming. This transition required planning. Throughout the years, she reminded all in her large family that she was preparing for her final journey. This was her last birthday, her last Easter, her last summer, her last Christmas. She was very matter-of-fact and not at all morbid in these pronouncements.

Sadly, I received a call telling me Mama had a stroke on her way home from the dentist. She collapsed in the street and was taken to Misericordia Hospital in the Bronx. Once there she remained in a coma for 13 days. There was no hope for survival. We had to wait until her strong little body weakened. Until her powerful heart could no longer do its work. Antonetta took her time. She did not leave us abruptly. She was preparing us for this profound separation. Her three sons had time to settle their differences. Children, grandchildren and friends took time being with her in the hospital; time for us to let her go. She was admitted to the hospital on March 18, 1982, and died on Saturday, April 10, 1982.

Mama taught me the ultimate lessons in loving and dying. On Good Friday I was alone with her. My husband, Charles, was understanding and cared for our two children all those hours I needed to be alone with her at the hospital. I had sensed she was ready. The time had come for me to say goodbye. The time had come to pray. I took her violet rosary beads. The old pair she always used, the rosary she repaired, sewing on the separated crucifix with white thread, making it whole again. I wrapped her rosary around our joined hands to pray our final prayers together. We were praying for her death. I could not believe this was happening – this was wrong, but it was right. I could feel her warmth, her reassurance. Her hands were like two furnaces.

The kisses and embraces had to last me for a long, long time. I am the baby, how could I lose my mother? Was she lost or in a newfound place? I left the hospital that night, not knowing what was going to happen. I felt a strange sense of closure and completeness. Mama taught me not to fear death. She taught me to face pain and death with courage and dignity.

The following day, Saturday, I received a telephone call from my brother, Lou. I knew what he was going to say. Mama had died. She died on Holy Saturday, the day before Easter Sunday. The one day of the year reserved for those saintly souls who, upon their death, travel directly to Heaven. This belief we were told by our Italian cousin, a priest, when the call was made with sad news of Mama's death. Don Angelo, our dear cousin and a Catholic priest, declared that Mama was blessed. He assured us she transitioned to Heaven. Hers was a quick flight to *Paradiso.*

The Funeral

As most serious-minded Italians, Mama planned her own funeral. The cemetery plot was ready with her lifetime partner. Papa waited six years for her to join him. Of course, the wake and funeral arrangements would be handled by the Romano Funeral Home on White Plains Road in the Bronx. The Mass would be at Saint Barnabas Church, her new parish, where she attended Mass every morning and was well known by the young priests. With careful forethought, the final plans were in place. However, I remembered that Mama was not quite sure which outfit to wear. Weeks before her death, I received a call. She told me the styles had changed, and maybe she should wear a long gown when she was "laid out." Of course, I would do anything she wanted. We made a date to go shopping. I was called a day later. Mama arrived a decision; she didn't need a new dress. This would only be a waste of money. Her burial outfit was "elegant." After all, it was the dress Grace (my sister) wore when Billy A (her son) married Vickie.

Knowing exactly where everything was in her closet, since she often showed me when I visited her, made things easier while we mourned. Mama prepared everything. Her wake was beautiful with a constant line of visitors including her grandchildren who crowded around her coffin touching her and giving her their final messages. On the day of the funeral Antonetta's children rode in a long black limousine and many cars followed.

On that Easter Monday morning, April 12, 1982, Paul played taps, and the large circle of family and friends mournfully sobbed their last farewell to Antonetta. My son Paul, the eleven-year-old bugler, proclaimed the closing blessing for his grandmother. She was gently buried at Woodlawn Cemetery in the Bronx, in the land of her good fortune, in the plot she lovingly maintained with springtime flowers and Christmas decorations.

You must understand for Italians; the whole funeral experience is quite an extravaganza. There is careful preparation of the body in the coffin to make a *bella figura*, good presentation. The coffin is carefully selected to reflect the status of the "dearly departed." Then comes the serious purchase of the flowers surrounding the casket at the funeral home. Have you ever seen the "Bleeding Heart" floral arrangement? It is quite something. It is a large (at least four or five feet in size) heart-shaped creation of red long-stemmed roses with many red satin ribbons (the blood) dripping down from the flowers.

Many other unique arrangements can only be designed and delivered by an expert florist well experienced in the needs of Italians facing the passing of a dear soul from earth to the spiritual realm. I particularly like the "blanket." This is a layer of flowers draped on the coffin, especially if those flowers are gardenias, which give one saying a prayer at the casket an uplifting sensory pause.

Next, the funeral mass with several priests celebrating, special music including the *Ave Maria*, and a bouquet of roses laid in honor of the Madonna. The cars are strategically organized outside the church for procession. Limos and a flower car are a must! Can you imagine a limo specially designed with an open section that visibly transports all those flowers to the burial site? The many cars show a proper sendoff. An old tradition is for the funeral procession to ride by the deceased's house as a farewell on the final pilgrimage to the cemetery. As you can imagine, a police escort is often required for such a motorcade.

Next, the cemetery. Now I must comment on the final resting place and the selection of the plot. Many Italians have already purchased a burial plot well before their death. My parents purchased a plot with friends at Wood-lawn where my sister Provie is interred. They felt secure in knowing their burial arrangements were made and this was one less burden for their children to deal with at the time of their death.

Sometimes a cemetery plot is to be selected by a young person having the Italian spirit and strongly sense of tradition. This is the case in our family when, to my surprise, our daughter, Meg, requested a plot for herself. When she was on a Christmas vacation, in her twenties at the time, we discussed possible Christmas gifts. She said, very matter-of-factly, "I would like a cemetery plot." We were startled by this different request from Santa. The decision was quickly made. Meg and my husband, Charles, drove to Gate of Heaven Cemetery in Hawthorne, New York, where many Magistro relatives were already buried. We asked our son, Paul, if he was interested in this family investment, but any preparation for death was not on his wish list. So, a four-person plot was purchased at the end of a beautiful lane close to other deceased family members.

When Meg returned to work after the school vacation and colleagues were discussing the presents they received for Christmas, Meg proudly announced her parents bought her a cemetery plot. You can just imagine the response from her non-Italian friends who shared lunch with her that day at Georgetown Day School. Of course, if they had come from an Italian family, they would have totally understood the generosity of this unusual Christmas gift from her parents.

Back to the funeral, after the burial and final farewell only food can help in the grieving process. A substantial dinner with ample alcoholic beverages goes a long way bringing us together to reminisce and cry together yet again. We know that soothing our need for nourishment and nurturance also makes sense even in this modern age.

How interesting that even today we repeat many of these behaviors in dealing with grief and loss in death. Sadly, it is not only when we face the death of an elderly family member or friend, but also when we must deal with the tragic death of loved ones who were much too young to die. Our need to make sense of life and understand the meaning of who we are and what matters in an often-chaotic world, intensifies our dependence on bonding with the traditions of the past.

Yes, I guess I am ready to finalize my plans. I write these words as I struggle with cancer. I need to be strong for my family. My love must find the courage Antonetta demonstrated for us. I can feel her embrace and am surrounded by her spirit. I am facing the reality of old age, illness, and death, but I think some traditions can be modified. What is meaningful for us changes. I continue to pray using Mama's violet rosary and call on Padre Pio for his assurances. Some old traditions remain important today. However, I can do without the fancy floral arrangements, but please keep the *Ave Maria*!

Antonetta has been an extraordinary presence and role model. The fearless Italian immigrant has taught us important life lessons and armed us with hope and love in gracefully facing life's challenges and the eventuality of our death.

POSTSCRIPT – ANTONETTA'S WILL

I have often asked family members for any document they may have in helping me write Antonetta's story. In May of 2025 after several attempts in searching my deceased brother Lou's files Carol, Lou's wife, called to say that she did find something Mama had written. Lou was the trusted anchor in our family, and everyone made sure to give him a copy of their will for safekeeping. I suspect that Lou was not able to read Italian and was probably not aware of the treasure he was given because he never mentioned her will to any of us. Did he even know what was thoughtfully and lovingly recorded on this simple piece of white stationery?

Antonetta wrote her will in November 1979. She died in April 1982. I shared her will with my brother George, my last surviving sibling, shortly after receiving it and together we interpreted her words and found that although we did not have this document at the time of her death her wishes were followed and honored. Together we felt her strong presence embracing us once more. We read her final words: *"I am your mother who gave you my good counsel and pray for you all Antonetta Lombardi."* The complete written document is included in Appendix G. In the final years of her life she became her own scribe, documenting her final wishes with love and the strength of her prayers for her children. Quite an amazing accomplishment for a woman having only a third-grade education.

APPENDIX A

LOMBARDI GENEALOGY

This genealogy chart begins with Antonio and Antonetta. They came to America without any relatives, and from these two parents, the Lombardi family now numbers more than 100.

PARENTS
Antonio Lombardi (1895-1976)
Antonia (Antonetta) Vincitorio Lombardi (1901-1982)

CHILDREN
Angelo, Grace, Michelina, Lucia, Providenza,
Louis, Antionette, George, Theresa

ANGELO (1921-2019) marries Millie Gambetta
Children: Lucille & Anthony
Lucille marries: Harold Boylan
Child: Michele
Michele marries: Bryan Chebetar
Great Grandchildren: Gabriella, Page, Alexandra
Lucille marries: Robert DeMeglio
Anthony marries Karen Burris
Children: Lauren, Katherine
Great Grandchildren: Matthew, Henry
Anthony's Partner: Judy Chernick

GRACE (1923-2013) marries Willian (Bill) Cornelius
Children: William (Billy A) & Margo (Mary Margaret)
Billy A marries Victoria Pella
Children: William (Billy T), Donna & Terri (twins), Alyssa
    (adopted)
Billy T marries Marianne Bollhofer
Great Grandchildren: Hailey, Alexandra, William
Terri marries Peter Arpia

Great Grandchildren: Ava, Gavin
Donna marries Peter Derasmo
Alyssa marries Gregory Billelo
Great Grandchildren: : Brielle, Lilah, Gregory
Margo Marries Howard Lorber
Children: Chelsea, Max
Chelsea marries Jamie Praeger
Great Grandchildren: Louisa, Jamie (JJ)
Max Marries: Melissa Fraser
Great Grandson: Miles

MICHELINA (1930-1931)

LUCIA (1931-1932)

PROVIDENZA (PROVIE, 1933-1958) marries Robert (Bob) Weiss
Children: Carey, Andrew
Carey marries Kevin Healy
Grandchildren: Christopher, William, Teressa
Christopher marries Daniel Thompson
Andrew marries Ellen Abrams
Grandchildren: Allison, Emily, Ava
Allison marries Andrew (Levine) Leveiss
Great Grandchildren: Lydia, Dean, Collette
Emily marries Alex Kluger
Great Grandchild: Julian
Ava marries Christian Verhulst
Naomi Weiss
Robert marries Olga Glassman
Child: Anne
Anne marries Eric Von Beck
Great Grandchild: Ajuna Fortuna (adopted from Ethiopia)

LOUIS (LOU, 1935-2020) marries Carol Ciavarella
Children: Louis, Linda, Steven, Susan, Carol Ann, George
Louis Jr. marries Mary Gurney

Grandchild: Alexa
Alexa marries Adam Sacramone
Great Grandchild: Meadow
Linda marries Cosmo Romeo
Grandchild: Nicole
Steven
Susan marries Kurt Freidhof
Great Grandchildren: Lauren, Alec
Lauren marries Santi Lara
Alec marries Hanna Cree
Carol Ann marries Henry Sung
Great Grandchildren: Tyler, Madison & Cameron (twins)
Geroge marries Christine Burns
Great Grandchildren: Lily, Jaden

ANTOINETTE (NAN, 1937-2024) marries Silas Seandel
Child: Marco
Marco marries Julia Grimes
Grandchild: Leo

GEORGE (1939-) marries Gina Monico
Children: Gabriella, Gian,
Gabriella marries James Wilday:
Great Grandchildren: Amelie, Benjamin & Lucia (twins)
Gian's Partner: Monique Gonzales
Great Grandchildren: Luca, Ella
George Marries: Antonia Racanelli

THERESA (1945-) marries Charles Magistro
Children: Paul, Margaret (Meg)
Paul marries Kathleen (Kate) Ruggles
Grandchildren: Isabel, Maisy, Charles (Charlie)
Meg marries Christopher (Chris) Arcadia
Grandchildren: Nicolas (Nico), Nina

Map of Italy
San Marco in Lamis, Province of Foggia

Appendix C

"San Marco in Lamis"[2]

The graveyard there on that worn slope, grass-fanned,
Thyme perfumed
Is bigger than the town, – a distant land,
Solemn, doomed.
Dark cypress – trees – (that land is Italy!),
Skyward, mute,
Long for no resurrection, so rock-deep
Is their root.

There each night, when the moon cannot peep through
Clouds and woods,
A nightingale that dares not sing for you
Sings on those roods,

Rustic, frost-bent. The melody I heard
As a child,
And it was then I thought of death as a bird
In the wild.

Had that bird crumbs more than I? I recall
I sang, too;
But after our same song, no bread at all
For us two.

Then morning rose – a rose from God to me,
Wonder-driven;
Squalid the walls, but festive were sky, sea –
We were even.

---

2 Joseph Tusiani, "San Marco in Lamis" in *Rind And All*. New York: The Monastine
Press, 1962): 49-52.

The sea was young, sail-dotted, rosy, white
Gold, green, blue –
My wonder adding all new shades of bright
Things untrue.

Soon I grew unaware of goat-bells shrill
In the street;
Of hands that watered basil on a sill;
Of clotheslines, wet

In the sun; of old vendors, early loud;
Of light asses
Mountainward, and of the soon swarming crowd
Of boys to classes,

And birds, those holiday birds though humble
Week. I was
Unaware of all things, yet the sweet rumble
Of all those

Spring hours was music too familiar
Not to hear
And love, though lost in song new and far
Was the ear.

Now I remember how life, like waves 'round
A stone hurled,
Revolved above a piece of holy ground,
The one world

Those peasants knew, those shepherds looked at, when
Passing by
With flock not their own, beneath the tent
Of the sky

And the escorting, pitying smile of the sun.
Now I know
Why, answering no question, asking none,
They must go,

Go on around the mountains that slope,
Grass caressed,
Taken them forever, folding their one hope
On its breast.

Shepherd, my little shepherd, is it true
You must roam,
As your father, from fall to fall till you,
Too, get home?

And it is true, old woman, frail and dry,
You must spin
Your wool just one year more till you can buy
A coffin,

And rest up there, in peace, leaving me no debt
And no name?
To be born, and rear children, then to settle
Down – this is fame.

The graveyard there on that worn slope, grass fanned,
Thyme-perfumed,
Is bigger than the town, – a distant land,
Solemn, doomed.

Theresa's Chronical to Her Siblings

Don Angelo's Funeral in San Marco in Lamis

DON ANGELO WAS A BELOVED PARISH PRIEST IN THE FAM-
ILY'S HOMETOWN OF SAN MARCO IN LAMIS, ITALY

*I received a call on Tuesday, September 26, 2006, that our
cousin, Don Angelo had died a few hours earlier. The pain of his
loss stayed with me throughout the night. Early the next morning
I called Meg and Paul to tell them the sad news. Thanks to Meg's
encouragement and the understanding of my need to be with our
cugini by both Charles and Paul, I hurriedly made arrangements
to go to Italy that late afternoon. Through a series of unusual circumstances, I arrived in San Marco on time for the service – a true
"miracle" declared by the cousins at my arrival. Papa would have
approved of my punctuality. I have written this chronicle to share
an important family event.*

DON ANGELO DONATO LOMBARDI
OCTOBER 9, 1911 – SEPTEMBER 26, 2006

On October 9, 1911, Don Angelo was born in his family
home in San Marco in Lamis, and died 95 years later at the
family summer residence, one mile up the mountain, in
Borgo Celano. Don Angelo's body was prepared at home by
Tonino, a parishioner of his church and a former member of
Don Angelo's scouting troop. He was laid in a wooden coffin and wrapped in a fine linen shroud edged in delicately
worked lace purchased in preparation for his burial many
years before by his sisters (Maria, Lucia, Michelina, and
Graciella).

The family had a few hours of private time before he
was taken in procession to his beloved church in the valley
with the sound of every church bell in the village ringing in

joyous celebration – in praise and honor of one who gave of himself to so many.

A Padre Pio Story

Zio Giuseppe, Papa's brother, visited Padre Pio in the neighboring town of San Giovanni in 1920. Upon receiving a candle given to him on behalf of the Lombardi family Padre Pio asked, "How is the little shepherd?" Zio Giuseppe, a farmer, answered, "Padre, I have no sheep." Padre Pio told him, "You have one at home who will be a Shepherd of Men." Don Angelo was nine years old and already preparing for his life's work as a Roman Catholic priest. This story was included in the eulogy preached by Archbishop Tamburrino Francesco Pio to a church full of family, friends, and brothers in Christ on September 28, 2006, in the sanctuary of San Antonio Abate in the town of San Marco in Lamis.

The story reminded me of the family journey many of us took in 1986 to San Marco in celebration of Don Angelo's 50th anniversary of ordination – of the memories we have of that trip and the beautiful sculpture of the Good Shepherd our brother-in-law Silas, Nan's husband, created for him.

The Funeral

On the day of Don Angelo's funeral I arrived at the church, San Antonio Abate on Corso Matteotti at two o'clock in the afternoon. I found a crowded church. The service was to begin at three. Don Angelo's body was lying in state since the day before. He was not taken to a funeral chapel as is our tradition in America. There I found Maria, Don Angelo's sister and her children praying at the altar. Before them on an exquisite oriental rug was Don Angelo's coffin placed on the floor of the church where he spent so many years of his ministry. I was told this unusual placement of the coffin was a planned precaution by the new pastor, Don Angelo's successor, because of the fear that so many would "Throw themselves in adoration." Adina (who was adopted into Maria's family when her children were young) announced that he was "laid out like a pope in Saint Peter's Basilica."

Don Angelo looked peaceful. He looked as though he had truly entered the realm of the divine. He was wearing the hand crocheted and embroidered vestment that Maria had spent two years creating for him when she was only 15 years old in preparation for his ordination. On top of this he wore a beautiful vestment given to him in celebration of his 70th anniversary of ordination by Maria's daughter Palmina and her Husband Nino. In his strong hands he held the golden chalice, a gift from all of Maria's children and grandchildren. At his feet was the carefully folded kerchief of the Sammarchese scouting troop he established and led for nearly five decades. Don Angelo was in his own church for a final farewell by hundreds who loved him. Looking down on him were the pastoral figures, the workers from "la piantura" – the agricultural community of Puglia – a mural he commissioned and personally paid for during the restoration of the old church San Antonio Abate.

Don Angelo's funeral was celebrated by 35 priests in addition to the Archbishop. Maria reminded me that night that we participated in 36 masses, one consecrated by each priest that day. The mass was sung by many voices of all ages including the spirited chants of a one-year-old child. The church was full. Father Don Ricciotti Saurino reminded the mourners to make room for the elderly, as there were not enough seats for all who came.

When the mass ended each person filed by the family to express their condolences in respect and gratitude. The receiving line took almost an hour. And in keeping with the

Italian tradition of two kisses, one on each cheek, it was impossible for me to count the number of kisses and embraces I received that afternoon, Don Angelo's coffin was then shut and draped with elegant white, long-stemmed roses for his last walk down the center aisle of San Antonio Abate. As his coffin was raised on the shoulder of six weeping men, the church vibrated in loud applause. A response I was not prepared for. He was carefully carried out of the church to a huge crowd singing in the street, a song Danielle (Grazia's son) later told me was one sung by scouts. A song sung at the end of an initiative when the scouts have reached their goal and the job is declared well done. Don Angelo's coffin was then placed in a shiny new black Mercedes Benz hearse. When the door was closed the crowd applauded again even louder than before with the sound of church bells ringing throughout the town.

The Cemetery

Many accompanied the family to the cemetery. The majority walked in silence through the town to their beloved cemetery. At the Lombardi family chapel, waiting for us with bricks, mortar, and a blowtorch were three laborers. The coffin was opened for a final blessing and an emotional family farewell. A steel plate was then soldered to the top of the steel-lined coffin, and the lid of the coffin was screwed in place. The coffin was carried to the vault to join his two sisters, Graciella and Michelina. Maria explained that he was supposed to be placed with his mother and father, Giuseppe and Archangela, but Lucia, his sister, who died in December 2005, had such an ornate coffin that the places had to be changed to accommodate her. After Don Angelo's coffin was placed in the vault, the workers came forward to seal it with bricks and mortar while the family witnessed the safe and careful placement of Don Angelo's precious remains. When all was completed at Matteo's (Maria's oldest son) signal we left the chapel to return to the family's summer home in Borgo Celano – the home where Don Angelo spent his final days of his life – the home filled with joyful memories of sumptuous meals and family pranks.

The Day After The Funeral

I am sitting here on Friday, September 29th, on the terrace in Borgo Celano, breathing in the clear, crisp fall air and embracing the warmth of the Pugliese sun, documenting these details for all of you who could not make this trip. Adina and Maria are in the kitchen preparing today's meal, carrying on the tradition of nurturing all those who come. I remember the summer of 1955, when Mama brought me here, where the strong bond and the love of our Italian roots were forever forged in me. I sit here connected to our beginning, to Mama and Papa. I close my eyes and revisit the stories they told us at the dinner table in the Bronx and spend the last few days with our cousins sharing the love of generations before I return home to America. America, our home, the land of opportunity, the land where Mama and Papa built their future, the land where we were raised with care and unconditional love that made us grow and prosper.

I was fortunate to have made this journey. And although I made it alone, I feel you are very much a part of all I experienced in these few days. I am sending you this chronicle of events from the last farewell to our Italian cousin, Don Angelo – one who had a lasting effect on us all.

I send you these words with love and affection, Theresa

Cousin Don Angelo Lombardi
San Marco in Lamis, Italy 1970

Grace Lombardi Cornelius

The "Write" of My Life

I have had many outstanding moments in my life but one of the most traumatic experiences was when I was six years old.

I was born in a small town in Italy, the province of Foggia, in the town of San Marco in Lamis, on the Adriatic Sea. One month after I was born my father left for America to make a better life for his family and to earn the money to pay for the passage of my mother, my brother, Angelo, and myself.

Finally, after six years this was accomplished and the long-awaited plans for our migration materialized. We left from the port of Naples on May 29, 1929.

As a child, many of the details were hazy, but one that I remember was that our townspeople, "paesans," would speak about the streets of America being paved with gold.

As we arrived in New York, there was fog and drizzle. Since most of the streets around the wharf were not paved, all we could see was dust and mud. I asked my mother where the gold streets were, and she was as disappointed as we all were, with no explanation.

The next memorable moment was when we met my father, who seemed very tall and handsome but a total stranger to me. I did not want to kiss him and hid under my mother's skirt. My brother, Angelo, was six years older than me, shook my father's hand but looked away very dubious.

From the ship, the "Conte Grande," we went to Ellis Island for inspection. There was a question about whether I would be allowed to enter because I had a yellow spot in my left eye. The Gods were with us, and I eventually got approved to enter. This was very frightening to me and I imagined being sent back to Italy alone. The yellow spot eventually disappeared but left the eye very weak.

From Ellis Island we took a ferry and then a subway up to the Bronx where we would make our home in a 3-room fifth floor walk-up apartment.

Right after our arrival home we were greeted by friends who also came from the same town. There was a lot of kissing and crying in the true Italian fashion.

One person, in particular, constantly asked me to speak so she could hear the Italian dialect from a child, which she found very amusing. I decided right then and there that I would hate this person the rest of my life for laughing at my expense.

Five months later the great depression was upon us and the rest is history.

My life has been many ups and downs but always full and interesting. For all my experiences since the age of six I came to realize that although the streets in America are not paved with gold this is still the greatest country on earth.

AUTHOR'S NOTE: This immigrant's story was written by my sister, Grace, when she was in her mid-seventies and attended a writing class in Toms River, New Jersey where she lived. She sent it to me at the time knowing I always treasured our family stories. Thank you, Grace.

The Reverend Dr. Charles Magistro officiating at
Carey & Kevin Healy's Wedding
New York City, 1985.

APPENDIX F

Antonetta's Eulogy
April 12, 1982

By her son-in-law, The Reverend Dr. Charles F. Magistro

*We meet here today in the presence of death to do homage to
the spirit of Life. We would like to make this hour Love's hour and
these rites Love's confessional. For it is Love's tribute that we
come to offer today.*

Our voices may be the voices of grief, but the language
after which grief gropes is the language of Love. And we
who gather here come in Love's name to express a calm
abiding trust in Love's immortality and consecrating
power.

"To everything there is a season," said the author of Ec-
cesiastes, "and a time for every purpose under Heaven.

A time to be born, and a time to die;

A time to plant, and a time to harvest;

A time to kill, and a time to heal;

A time to break, and a time to build;

A time to weep, and a time to laugh;

A time to mourn, and a time to dance;

A time to cast away stones, and a time to bring stones
together;

A time to embrace, and a time to be apart;

A time to get and a time to lose;

A time to keep silence, and a time to speak

Few knew this better than Mama. She responded to life
as the occasion required. She understood that tragedy and
triumph come to us all, that life both pains and uplifts,

- 141 -

wounds and heals, shatters and concentrates. More importantly, however, she possessed the serenity to accept the things she could not change, the courage to change the things she could, and the wisdom to know the difference.

Mama was a truly remarkable woman. Her life was a magnificent success! Her spirit was more than equal to fate and fortune. For she not only rose to the occasion but above it. She possessed an inner strength, and a quiet self-confidence, an indefatigable faith that inspired and sustained us. She nurtured us, worked for us, prayed for us. She loved us without judging us and rooted us without limiting us. She made us one family and, at the same time, affirmed us as individuals whose uniqueness, dignity, and worth were always beyond question. In short, she was what each of us needed her to be. And we can only wonder, in heartfelt gratitude, as to the source of nobility and grandeur of spirit.

From whence came her wisdom and insight and unobtrusive determination to vouchsafe our happiness, her steadfastness and grit and unbounded generosity, her fortitude in the face of hardship, her optimism in the face of tragedy, her confidence in people in the face of human limitations?

The answer is by no means obvious. Her life, like the lives of many of her friends, was one of unrelenting struggle. But she knew more than poverty and deprivation; she knew the pain of irredeemable disappointment and the trauma of personal loss as well.

She was orphaned at eight. Was left in Italy to rear Angelo and Grace while Papa sought to establish a new life for their family in the United States. She arrived on these shores on the eve of the Great Depression. She spent the prime of her life in mortal combat with the fears and vicissitudes that threaten life.

She outlived three of her children – one of whom was a grown woman with children of her own. She saw her husband of a lifetime through a painful and protracted death. But she knew the hurts and disappointments too deep to speak. She never complained about her lot in life. She was seemingly without anger or bitterness or cynicism. On the contrary, she affirmed the goodness of life with every breath she took. Like Job, she refused to curse her God. But neither did she passively submit to the will of God as an inexorable fate. Rather, she redeemed even the apparently irredeemable by making the best that could be made of any particular circumstance or event. Such was the power of her love and faith, of her presence in and to life, of her sense of self and the meaningfulness of her existence. Mama was our strength and in adversity and comfort in distress. She was our inspiration. She was our mother.

And she loved being our mother. Her nature was to nurture. But if she blessed our lives, if she took pride, not merely in our accomplishments, but in ourselves as persons, we were also a blessing to her. For we loved her and honored her and respected her with a respect that bordered on reverence; and in our love, honor and respect she found sufficient justification for the sacrifices of a lifetime. Our happiness as individuals and harmony as a family were, not just important, but central to what she saw as the significance of having lived.

Antonetta at 81 Years of Age, Yonkers, NY 1982

ANTONETTA'S WILL, written on November 23, 1979

Li 23 novembre 1979
figli tutti io vi scrivo questo figlietto
per dirvi tutto quando io more così
non fate lito, nella casa come sta
compilita, tutti li picci fotografie a
chi la partenca li passono pigliare, poi
ci sta li quatri del vostro padre e fatto la
prima guerra o chi li piace per ricordo
ci li pigliano il quadro col gole di oro
del funirore e di giorgi, che a fatto tutto per
vendere la casa e non avuto niende, fa ma-
china singere per cucire e di Teresa, li rica-
di di quando abbiamo fatto 50 di madrimo-
no ci li può pigliare chi ci la dato, e il
resto che ci avete fatto per il talivisione
e la tavolo per mangiare io vi li do prima
che Dio mi chiama, e tutto che ci resto e di
Furnitura e di Luigi giugno Lombardi
la moneta che sta nella banga mi fatti fate
il Funerale li stesse pasto Roma e come a fatto
al vostro, e ci o la vesta nella scatole e tutto per
vestire, ma la vesta mi lovete comprare semplice

ci ho 1000 tollari di sicurazione, e 250
tollari di zuguriti che tutto La spettano,
e 4 miladollari che stallo alla banga
pagato tutto, e ci restano vili spaccito,

 e dopo vi facita un bel pranzo
e noi pregliamo per voi tutti così
Di vi aiuta

 e sono la mamma di vi ho dato
buona guida
  pregliate per tutti
  Antonetta Lombardi

ABOUT THE AUTHOR

THERESA LOMBARDI MAGISTRO is a Bronx baby born to Italian immigrants from the Puglia region, the ninth and last child in a close-knit family. She was educated in the New York City Public Schools and graduated from The City College of New York of The City of New York in 1967. Theresa taught in the field of special education for over 30 years, working at all levels. She was elected president of the Stamford Education Association, implementing changes on a broad scale. Active in her community, she served as a Commissioner on the Urban Redevelopment Commission in Stamford, Connecticut, for 12 years, where she was an advocate for pedestrian enhancements in the downtown area. Married and the mother of two children and five grandchildren, Theresa lives in New Providence, New Jersey. This memoir is her first book.

Photo by Carey Weiss

Theresa Magistro
Email: tlmagistro@gmail.com